Spiritual Warfare/Deliverance
Handbook 101

Scripture taken from the King James Version, New International Version, and The Message Bible or as otherwise listed in book via Biblegateway.com.

You may contact the author at: info@karenLhill.com

TABLE OF CONTENTS

Foreword

Karen Hill is an author, prophetic prayer warrior and a dynamic teacher of the word of God. Under the direction of the Holy Spirit, she has penned a book that explains the practical side of the ministry of deliverance. The Bible refers to it as the casting out of demons. This term frightens many Christians; as a result, they shy away from the subject of deliverance. Minister Hill brings clarity to this issue.

Many members of the body of Christ do not understand the power of deliverance or the relevance of its application in our lives as a tool for sanctification. Jesus said deliverance is the children's bread making it clear to us that as a child of God; deliverance must be a part of our spiritual diet. Many believers, even pastors, do not believe that a Christian can be affected by demonic activity. A study of the scriptures will prove otherwise.

Demonic activity occurs in the flesh or mind of a person. The born-again spirit cannot be inhabited by demons, but the work of the spirit is hindered as the mind or flesh is under torment. The way I like to say it is, "Christians cannot be possessed by a demon. They can however be oppressed by them." The spiritual weapon of casting out demons effectively helps a Christian find great victory over habits and strongholds in their lives. The key is understanding the work of demons (2 Corinthians 2:11), how they attempt to control and limit the godly actions of a believer and how to use the word of God to render them useless in their efforts.

Karen Hill, through years of prayer, study of the word and the experience of ministering deliverance, has become qualified to share with you keys of how to attain victory and how to walk in your God given spiritual authority. I applaud her obedience to the Holy Spirit in writing this book. Use it as a manual for deliverance.

Apostle Cedric Taylor
Memphis, Tennessee

CHAPTER 1

Spiritual Warfare –

What Is It All About?

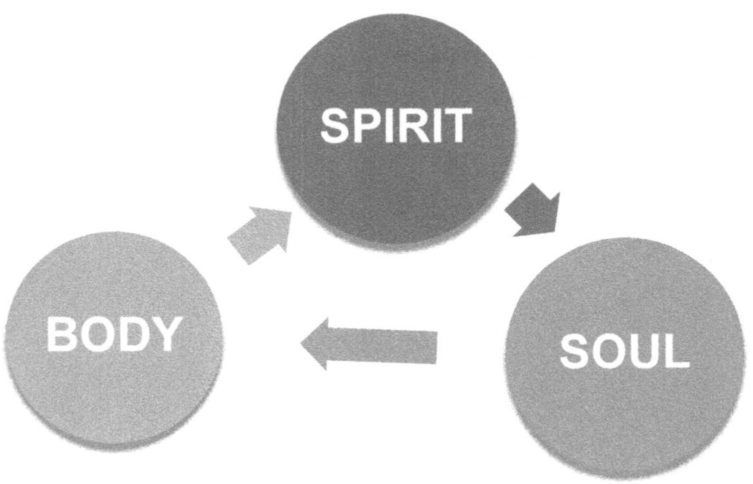

May God himself, the God who makes everything holy and whole, make you holy and whole, put you together - spirit, soul, and body - and keep you fit for the coming of our Master, Jesus Christ. The One who called you is completely dependable. If he said it, he'll do it! *I Thess. 5:23-24 (MSG)*

Spiritual Warfare - What Is It All About?

As humans, we are more prone to focus on what we can see rather than what we cannot see and spiritual warfare is a conflict we cannot see. However, the Bible strongly suggests that the unseen world has and will always continue to have a profound effect on both the world in which we live and the hereafter. So we must learn as much as we can about both worlds and gain a better understanding of what is going on "behind the scenes".

As believers, we have been thrust into an invisible fight that starts in the spiritual realm but is very much seen and felt in the visible (physical world). Therefore, an understanding of spiritual things is a must for the believer. Now more than ever, God wants his people to pay more attention to spiritual matters because the physical world in which we live is subject to the spiritual realm and we must learn to successfully maneuver in both worlds.

While we look not at the things which are seen, but at the things which are not seen: for the things which are seen are temporal; but the things which are not seen are eternal. 2 Corinthians 4:18 (KJV)

First Things First - Believing in the Things We Cannot See

Warfare includes the discussion of three (3) important spiritual components: Man, God and Satan.

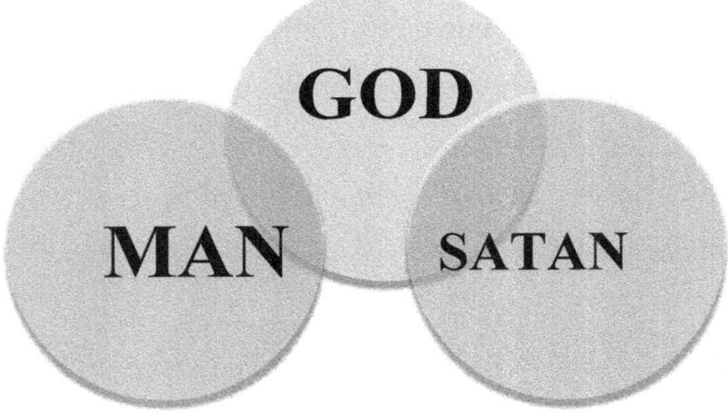

I. God created man and there are three (3) points we should consider regarding his existence. Man is a three part being – Spirit, Body and Soul.

a) We cannot see our Spirit – the consciousness, life and source of power that should be controlling the body and soul. The Bible states "God is a Spirit" and "we are created in His image". The spirit is the God part of us. It connects us to God, helps us to communicate with God and helps us to walk in His Spirit.

[26a] And God said, Let us make man in our image, after our likeness: ...[27] So God created man in his own image, in the image of God created he him; male and female created he them.
Gen. 1:26-27 (KJV)

[7]Then shall the dust return to the earth as it was: and the spirit shall return unto God who gave it. Ecclesiastes 12:7 (KJV)

b) We can see and touch our Bodies – the physical characteristics of who we are. We are convinced we have bodies because we can see, feel and touch our bodies.

[19] In the sweat of thy face shalt thou eat bread, till thou return unto the ground; for out of it wast thou taken: for dust thou art, and unto dust shalt thou return. Gen. 3:19 (KJV)

c) We cannot see our Soul – the core of our reasoning, intellect, desires and intentions. It is the life of the body. Human souls all have unique personalities, emotions and a will.

[7]And the LORD God formed man of the dust of the ground, and breathed into his nostrils the breath of life; and man became a living soul. Gen. 2:7 (KJV)

II. God is the self-existent one and creator. There are three (3) points we should consider regarding His existence. The fact that we cannot see God does not mean He doesn't exist.

---

a) God is God regardless of whether or not you can see and touch Him. He is all-powerful and perfect in every way.

[24] This is what the Lord says - your Redeemer, who formed you in the womb: "I am the Lord, who has made all things, who alone stretched out the heavens, who spread out the earth by myself. . ." Isaiah 44:24 (NIVI)

[1] The fool says in his heart, "There is no God"... Psalm 14:1 (NIVI)

b) The very design implies a designer.

[16] For by Him all things were created: things in heaven and on earth, visible and invisible, whether thrones or powers or rulers or authorities: all *things have been created through Him and for Him. [17] He is before all things, and in Him all things hold together. Colossians 1:16-17 (NIV)*

[1] In the beginning God created the heavens and the earth. [2] Now the earth was formless and empty, darkness was over the surface of the deep, and the Spirit of God was hovering over the waters. Genesis 1:1-2 (NIV)

[25] In the beginning you laid the foundations of the earth, and the heavens are the work of your hands. Psalm 102:25 (NIV)

c) Everyone has an inner knowledge of God.

[20] For since the creation of the world God's invisible qualities - his eternal power and divine nature - have been clearly seen, being understood from what has been made, so that people are without excuse. Romans 1:20 (NIV)

III. God is the creator of Satan. There are three (3) points we should consider regarding his existence. We cannot see Satan but we know he exists.

---

a) Satan is an angel created by God who rebelled against God.

[1] Now the serpent was more subtil than any beast of the field which the Lord God had made. And he said unto the woman, Yea, hath God said, Ye shall not eat of every tree of the garden? Genesis 3:1 (KJV)

b) Satan exists whether or not you can see or touch him.

[44] Ye are of your father the devil, and the lusts of your father ye will do. He was a murderer from the beginning, and abode not in the truth, because there is no truth in him. When he speaketh a lie, he speaketh of his own: for he is a liar, and the father of it. John 8:44 (KJV)

c) Satan is described as the ruler of this world and is responsible for the oppression, depression, stress, confusion, frustration and failure of mankind.

[8] *Be of sober spirit, be on the alert. Your adversary, the devil, prowls around like a roaring lion, seeking someone to devour.* [9] *But resist him, firm in your faith, knowing that the same experiences of suffering are being accomplished by your brethren who are in the world. 1 Peter 5:8-9 (NASB)*

The acceptances of these three (3) basic truths are the foundation for Spiritual Warfare/Deliverance Handbook 101.

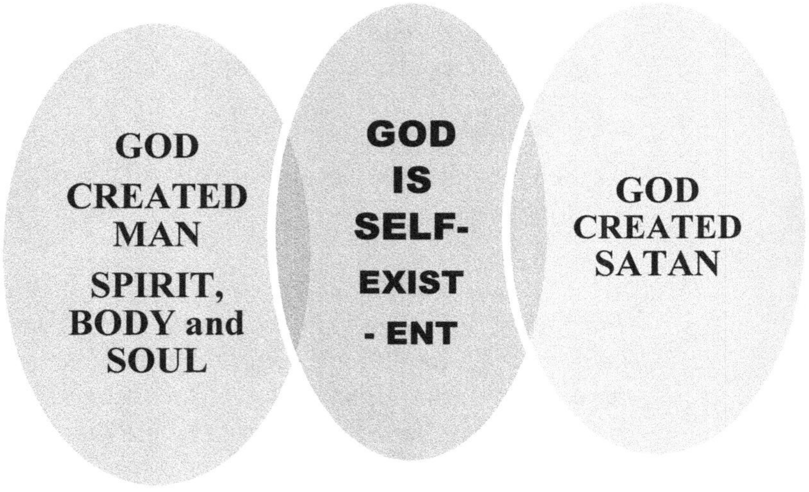

GOD CREATED MAN SPIRIT, BODY and SOUL

GOD IS SELF-EXIST - ENT

GOD CREATED SATAN

SPIRITUAL WARFARE DEFINED

1) Spiritual Warfare is "a conflict between two opposing wills" (the kingdom of Satan and the kingdom of God). Source: Spiritual Warfare, Biblical Truth for Victory, John Franklin and Chuck Lawless, Lifeway Press, Nashville, Tennessee

When Does Spiritual Warfare Begin?

Spiritual warfare began before we were born, historically, generationally and personally, before we were developed in the womb. For the Bible says, "*Behold, I was shapen in iniquity; and in sin did my mother conceive me Psalm 51:5 (KJV).* We become more conscious of this fight when we become saved, and increasingly more aware as we mature in Christ. The truth of the matter is - we come into this world scrapping by and don't even know it. At some point, even the unsaved begin to have some awareness and wherewithal to know that something is affecting their world, environment and their personal circumstances beyond what they are able to see. Once Christians are taught the word of God, all the pieces of the puzzle begin to come together. We choose to either become more effective players, by doing what it takes to fight effectively and win or we buckle and succumb to defeat.

1) Once we are saved, we become a part of the Kingdom of God
2) Die to self - we surrender body and soul to the control of the spirit

3) Fight in the spirit - we no longer engage in physical battles (boxing gloves and guns serve no purpose in gaining victory over life's problems)

Who Is Involved in Spiritual Warfare?

There are two parties involved in this conflict:

1) Satan and his followers
    a. Satan wants evil and encourages wrong
    b. Satan destroys
    c. Satan represents what is corrupt and perverse

2) God and his children
    a. God is good and wants good things for his children
    b. God builds and does not tear down
    c. God represents what is pure and holy

Spiritual Warfare

Satan+Followers

God + Children

Source: Spiritual Warfare, Biblical Truth for Victory, John Franklin and Chuck Lawless, Lifeway Press, Nashville, Tennessee

Who Initiated This War?

The conflict between the opposing forces was initiated by Satan.

Who Is Satan?

1) Satan was a holy angel created by God (Ezekiel 28:12-15)

2) Satan was very powerful and very wise (wisdom & beauty) (Ezekiel 28:12)

3) Satan was an angel who rebelled against God (Isaiah 14:13-14)

4) Satan was permanently removed from his position because of pride (Isaiah 14:12-15)

5) Satan is the god of this world and the prince of the power of the air (2 Cor. 4:4, Eph. 2:2)

Satan's intent toward God is identified in scripture

13) For you have said in your heart: I will ascend into heaven, I will exalt my throne above the stars

of God; I will also sit on the mount of the congregation on the farthest sides of the north;
14) I will ascend above the heights of the clouds, I will be like the Most High. Isaiah 14:13-14 (NKJV)

When and Where Did Warfare Begin?

A War Took Place in Heaven

7) And there was war in heaven: Michael and his angels fought against the dragon; and the dragon fought and his angels, 8) And prevailed not; neither was their place found any more in heaven.
9) And the great dragon was cast out, that old serpent, called the Devil, and Satan, which deceiveth the whole world: he was cast out into the earth, and his angels were cast out with him. Revelation 12:7-9 (KJV)

During this war, Satan was cast to the earth and his angels with him

About the angels that were cast out with Satan:

- ✓ When Satan fell, he drew a third of the angels with him (Revelation 12:4,9)

- ✓ Some of the fallen angels are loose (known as demons) and some are bound in a place called the Abyss (Luke 8:31)
- ✓ Satan and his demons are still waging war against the Kingdom of God (Revelation 12:17)
- ✓ Satan now dwells on earth (Job 1:7)
- ✓ At the second coming of Christ, Satan will be bound for 1,000 years (Revelation 20:1-3)
- ✓ After the thousand years, Satan will be set free for a short time and will go out to deceive the nations (Revelation 20:7-9)
- ✓ Satan's final end will be in the Lake of Fire, which was prepared by God for him and his angels (Revelation 20:10, Matthew 25:41)

How Long Will the Battle Continue?

The conflict between good and evil will rage until Satan is destroyed *(Rev. 20:7).*

Our Battle is not with Humans

For we wrestle not against flesh and blood, but against principalities, against powers, against the rulers of the darkness of this world, against spiritual wickedness in high places. Ephesians 6:12 (KJV)

How Important is it for Warfare to Continue?

1) Warfare continues or ceases based on whether or not God's purpose is accomplished Source: Spiritual Warfare, Biblical Truth for Victory, John Franklin and Chuck Lawless, Lifeway Press, Nashville, Tennessee
2) God uses warfare to accomplish His will *(John 13:27)*
3) God does not exempt His children from conflict
4) Remember Good vs. Evil (God builds – Satan destroys)
5) When we become believers, we do not instantly become perfect and spiritually mature
6) Christ demonstrated that we can win against Satan and He equipped us to evolve and follow His example; thereby, gaining victory in the conflict that exists between the two kingdoms

If we don't give up, we will rule with him. If we deny that we know him, he will deny that he knows us. (2 Timothy 2:12) CEV)

And hast made us unto our God kings and priests: and we shall reign on the earth. (Revelation 5:9-11)(KJV)

God has a plan for us to grow and mature in Him *(Jeremiah 29:11)* and Satan is granted permission from

God to act in the life of the believer *(Job 1:6-12; 2:1-6, Luke 22:31-32)*

EXAMPLES OF SPIRITUAL WARFARE IN ACTION

EXAMPLE (A) - SATAN'S STRATEGIES AGAINST JOB

Strategy #1 – Satan obtains permission from God to test Job

> *6) Now there was a day when the sons of God came to present themselves before the Lord, and Satan came also among them. 7) And the Lord said unto Satan, Whence comest thou? Then Satan answered the Lord, and said, From going to and fro in the earth, and from walking up and down in it. 8) And the Lord said unto Satan, Hast thou considered my servant Job, that there is none like him in the earth, a perfect and an upright man, one that feareth God, and escheweth evil? Job 1:6-8 (NJV)*
>
> *And the LORD said unto Satan, Behold, all that he hath is in thy power; only upon himself put not*

forth thine hand. So Satan went forth from the presence of the LORD. Job 1:12 (NJV)

1) Again there was a day when the sons of God came to present themselves before the LORD, and Satan came also among them to present himself before the LORD. 2) And the LORD said unto Satan, From whence comest thou? And Satan answered the LORD, and said, From going to and fro in the earth, and from walking up and down in it.
3) And the LORD said unto Satan, Hast thou considered my servant Job, that there is none like him in the earth, a perfect and an upright man, one that feareth God, and escheweth evil? and still he holdeth fast his integrity, although thou movedst me against him, to destroy him without cause. 4) And Satan answered the LORD, and said, Skin for skin, yea, all that a man hath will he give for his life. 5) But put forth thine hand now, and touch his bone and his flesh, and he will curse thee to thy face. 6) And the LORD said unto Satan, Behold, he is in thine hand; but save his life. Job 2: 1-6 (KJV)

Strategy #2 – Satan launches a personal attack on Job's Character

9) Then Satan answered the LORD, and said, Doth Job fear God for nought?
10) Hast not thou made an hedge about him, and about his house, and about all that he hath on every side? thou hast blessed the work of his

hands, and his substance is increased in the land. 11) But put forth thine hand now, and touch all that he hath, and he will curse thee to thy face. Job 1:9-11 (KJV)

4) And Satan answered the LORD, and said, Skin for skin, yea, all that a man hath will he give for his life. 5) But put forth thine hand now, and touch his bone and his flesh, and he will curse thee to thy face. Job 2:4-5 (KJV)

Strategy #3 – Satan launches an attack on Job's Finances

His substance also was seven thousand sheep, and three thousand camels, and five hundred yoke of oxen, and five hundred she asses, and a very great household; so that this man was the greatest of all the men of the east. Job 1:3 (KJV)

14) And there came a messenger unto Job, and said, The oxen were plowing, and the asses feeding beside them: 15) And the Sabeans fell upon them, and took them away; yea, they have slain the servants with the edge of the sword; and I only am escaped alone to tell thee. 16) While he was yet speaking, there came also another, and said, The fire of God is fallen from heaven, and hath burned up the sheep, and the servants, and consumed them; and I only am escaped alone to tell thee. 17) While he was yet speaking, there came also another, and said, The Chaldeans made out three bands, and fell upon the camels, and have carried them away, yea, and slain the servants with the edge of the sword; and I only am escaped alone to tell thee. Job 1:14-17 (KJV)

Strategy #4 – Satan launches an attack on Job's Family

18) While he was yet speaking, there came also another, and said, Thy sons and thy daughters were eating and drinking wine in their eldest brother's house: 19) And, behold, there came a great wind from the wilderness, and smote the four corners of the house, and it fell upon the young men, and they are dead; and I only am escaped alone to tell thee. Job 1:18-19 (KJV)

Strategy #5 – Satan launches an attack on Job's Health

1) Again there was a day when the sons of God came to present themselves before the Lord, and Satan came also among them to present himself before the Lord. 2) And the Lord said unto Satan, From whence comest thou? And Satan answered the Lord, and said, From going to and fro in the earth, and from walking up and down in it. 3) And the Lord said unto Satan, Hast thou considered my servant Job, that there is none like him in the earth, a perfect and an upright man, one that feareth God, and escheweth evil? and still he holdeth fast his integrity, although thou movedst me against him, to destroy him without cause. 4) And Satan answered the Lord, and said, Skin for skin, yea, all that a man hath will he give for his life. 5) But put forth thine hand now, and touch his bone and his flesh, and he will curse thee to thy face. 6) And the Lord said unto Satan, Behold, he is in thine hand; but save his life. Job 2:1-6 (KJV)

Strategy #6 – Satan launches an attack on Job's Faith/Beliefs

8) And the Lord said unto Satan, Hast thou considered my servant Job, that there is none like him in the earth, a perfect and an upright man, one that feareth God, and escheweth evil? 9) Then Satan answered the Lord, and said, Doth Job fear God for nought?
Job 1:8-9 (KJV)

And the Lord said unto Satan, Hast thou considered my servant Job, that there is none like him in the earth, a perfect and an upright man, one that feareth God, and escheweth evil? and still he holdeth fast his integrity, although thou movedst me against him, to destroy him without cause. Job 2:3 (KJV)

Then said his wife unto him, Dost thou still retain thine integrity? curse God, and die. Job 2:9 (KJV)

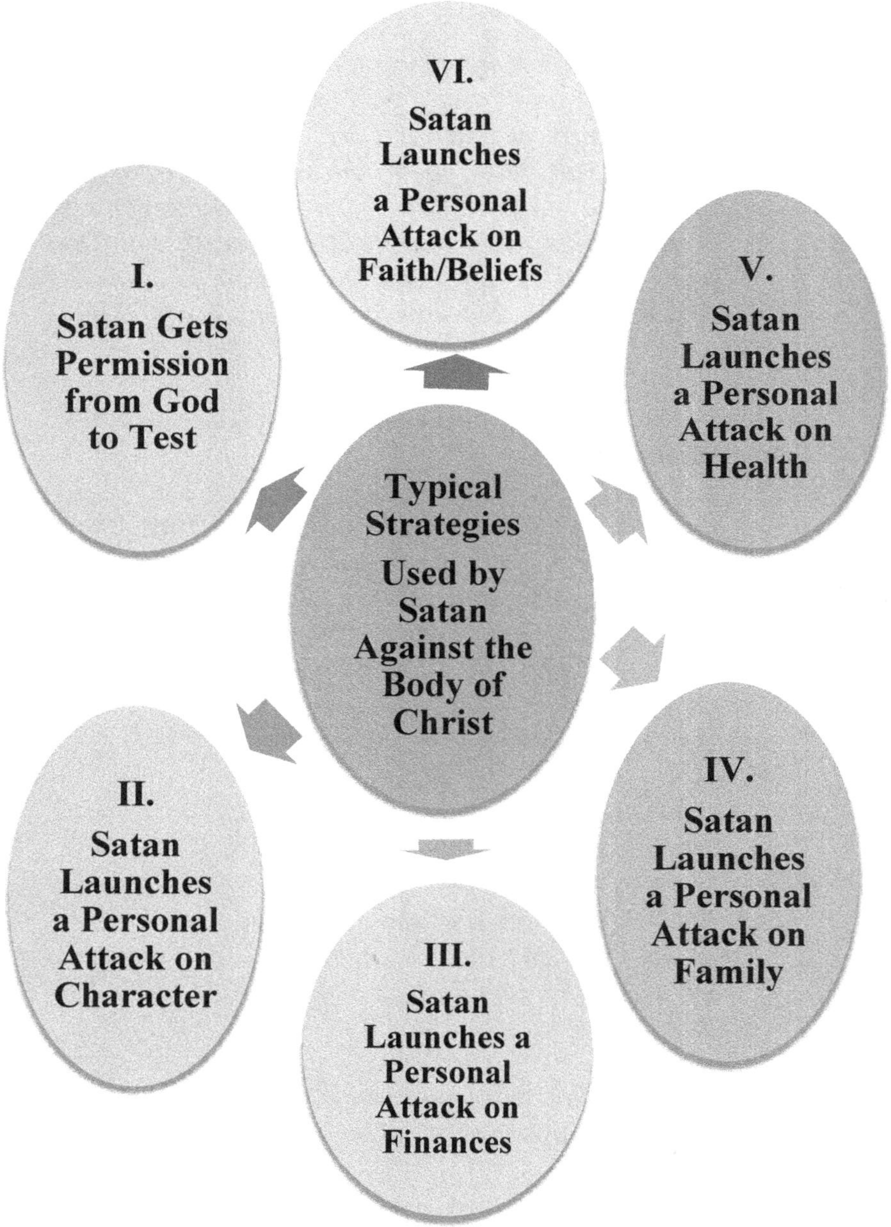

Typical Strategies Used by Satan Against the Body of Christ

I.
Satan Gets Permission from God to Test

II.
Satan Launches a Personal Attack on Character

III.
Satan Launches a Personal Attack on Finances

IV.
Satan Launches a Personal Attack on Family

V.
Satan Launches a Personal Attack on Health

VI.
Satan Launches a Personal Attack on Faith/Beliefs

EXAMPLE (B) – SATAN'S STRATEGIES AGAINST PETER (AS WARNED BY JESUS)

1. We can assume that Satan received permission for testing Peter

31) And the Lord said, Simon, Simon, behold, Satan hath desired to have you, that he may sift you as wheat: 32) But I have prayed for thee, that thy faith fail not: and when thou art converted, strengthen thy brethren. 33) And he said unto him, Lord, I am ready to go with thee, both into prison, and to death. 34) And he said, I tell thee, Peter, the cock shall not crow this day, before that thou shalt thrice deny that thou knowest me. Luke 22:31-34 (KJV)

2. Peter made a choice to lie and failed his test.

55) And when they had kindled a fire in the midst of the hall, and were set down together, Peter sat down among them. 56) But a certain maid beheld him as he sat by the fire, and earnestly looked upon him, and said, This man was also with him. 57) And he denied him, saying, Woman, I know him not. 58) And after a little while another saw him, and said, Thou art also of them. And Peter said, Man, I am not. 59) And about the space of one hour after another confidently affirmed, saying, Of a truth this fellow also was with him: for he is a Galilaean. 60) And Peter said, Man, I know not what thou sayest. And immediately, while he yet spake, the cock crew. 61) *And the Lord turned, and looked upon Peter. And Peter remembered the word of the Lord, how he had said unto him, Before the cock crow, thou shalt deny me thrice. Luke 22:55-61 (KJV)*

3. Peter repented

4. Jesus prayed for Peter and consequently Peter became victorious

5. Peter and the other disciples turned the world upside down preaching Jesus Christ.

EXAMPLE (C) – WARFARE AFFECTS EVERYONE – EVEN PAUL

I will say this: because these experiences I had were so tremendous, God was afraid I might be puffed up by them; so I was given a physical condition which has been a thorn in my flesh, a messenger from Satan to hurt and bother me and prick my pride. 2 Corinthians 12:7 (TLB)

There are examples in the New Testament where Satan used various attacks against Paul. They will not be mentioned here, but we learn that even Paul had to realize the battle was not his but God's.

> *5) I will boast about someone like that, but I will not boast about myself, except about my weaknesses. 6) Even if I should choose to boast, I would not be a fool, because I would be speaking the truth. But I refrain, so no one will think more of me than is warranted by what I do or say, 7) or because of these surpassingly great revelations. Therefore, in order to keep me from becoming conceited, I was given a thorn in my flesh, a messenger of Satan, to torment me. 8) Three times I pleaded with the Lord to take it away from me. 9) But he said to me, "My grace is sufficient for you, for my power is made perfect in weakness." Therefore I will boast all the more gladly about my weaknesses, so that Christ's power may rest on me. 10) That is why, for Christ's sake, I delight in weaknesses, in insults, in hardships, in persecutions, in difficulties. For when I am weak, then I am strong. 2 Corinthians 12:5-10 (TNIV)*

WHAT TO REMEMBER REGARDING WARFARE

Remember Satan is limited. Satan has no power except what he is given by God. It is God who directs the affairs of the world.

1) Things do not randomly happen to the children of God.
2) God uses the circumstances in our lives for His greater purpose.
3) God is sovereign and our battle is His; therefore, we cannot be defeated.

HOW SHOULD WE HANDLE WARFARE

I. Take comfort in the word of God

1) There is a way of escape from temptation (I Corinthians 10:13)
2) Count it all joy (James 1:2)
3) Lay aside every weight (Hebrews 12:1-3)
4) Overcome evil with good (Romans 12:21)
5) Know that Satan is already defeated (I John 3:8-9)
6) We win (Matthews 16-18)

II. Do not follow Job's initial reaction to his testing – Job had a pity party

After this opened Job his mouth, and cursed his day. Job 3:1 (KJV)

For the thing which I greatly feared is come upon me and that which I was afraid of is come unto me. Job 3:25 (NJV)

Man that is born of a woman is of few days and full of trouble. Job 14:1 (KJV)

III. Do follow Job's final response to testing, which produced a victorious climax

And the Lord turned the captivity of Job, when he prayed for his friends: also the Lord gave Job twice as much as he had before. Job 42:10 (KJV)

IV. Do follow Peter's example after repentance?

After Peter denied Christ three times, he repented. Unlike many Christians, he did not alienate himself from the saints for his faithlessness and weakness but leaned into the word and his faith. He later appeared at the resurrection of Christ, preached the Pentecost message and traveled widely preaching the gospel to the Jews and Gentiles and converting people to Christianity. Peter did exactly as he was admonished by Jesus Christ to do. He set about to strengthen the brethren.

V. Do follow Paul's example

1) Paul worked many signs and wonders and traveled widely to take the gospel to the Gentiles. Paul went on to write the largest portion of the New Testament.

2) He also established churches and was remembered as one of the greatest Christian leaders of our times.

VI. Let us be patient

2) Consider it pure joy, my brothers and sisters, whenever you face trials of many kinds, 3) because you know that the testing of your faith produces perseverance. 4) Let perseverance finish its work so that you may be mature and complete, not lacking anything. James 1:2-4 (NIV)

In other words, when the work of patience is complete, it will accomplish all that is necessary for successful warfare. Let's catch hold to the concept of patience and utilize it in our daily lives. Stand firm.

1) Wherefore seeing we also are compassed about with so great a cloud of witnesses, let us lay aside every weight, and the sin which doth so easily beset us, and let us run with patience, the race that is set before us, 2) Looking unto Jesus the author and finisher of our faith; who for the joy that was set before him endured the cross, despising the shame, and is set down at the right hand of the throne of God. 3) For consider him that endured such contradiction of sinners against himself, lest ye be wearied and faint in your minds. Hebrews 12:1-3 (KJV)

THERE IS GOOD NEWS!

Satan is already defeated

Having disarmed principalities and powers, He made a public spectacle of them, triumphing over them in it. Colossians 2:15 (NKJV)

Satan's ultimate end

The devil, who deceived them, was cast into the lake of fire and brimstone where the beast and the false prophet are. And they will be tormented day and night forever and ever. Revelation 20:10 (NKJV)

GOD WILL AID HIS CHILDREN IN SPIRITUAL WARFARE

1) The battle is the Lord's. He will give it into our hands - 1 Samuel 17:47
2) Do not be afraid of the multitude, the battle is the Lord's – 2 Chron. 20:15
3) Count it joy when temptations/trouble comes – James 1:2
4) You will not be tempted above what you are able to withstand – I Cor. 10:13
5) All things work together for good to them that love God and are called – Romans 8:28
6) After you have suffered a little while, God will make you perfect, stablish, strengthen and settle you – I Peter 5:10
7) Lay aside every weight and sin that easily besets and run with patience – Hebrews 12:1

CHAPTER 2

Weapons of Spiritual Warfare

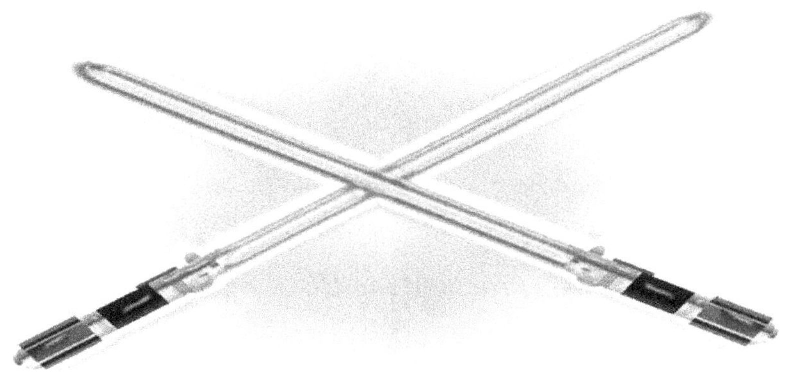

"The weapons we fight with are not the weapons of the world. On the contrary, they have divine power to demolish strongholds." *2 Corinthians 10:4 (NIV)*

Weapons of Spiritual Warfare

God has provided numerous weapons for us to use in this spiritual battle. While natural weapons are of no use, God has amply supplied enough arsenals to keep us fully engaged and winning. Like any army, one must be trained to fight and defeat the enemy to avoid becoming a casualty of war. Subsequently, we demonstrate in the physical realm the victory already won for us at the cross.

Exactly which weapon to use will depend on the type of warfare one is facing. A well trained soldier will have knowledge of all of his weapons and with time will definitely have the opportunity to use some, if not all, of his weapons. Subsequently, he will find the weapons most advantageous to him and use them well. A good soldier, like any successful army, must be trained and tested.

God uses Warfare to Move His Kingdom Forward

1) When we become believers, we do not automatically become perfected – mature saints

2) We must grow in God. God allows warfare to play a part in that growth

3) This warfare draws us to the face of God where He provides needed assistance

Warfare – Is a type of Refiner's Fire

There is nothing done to you that God does not give the enemy (Satan) permission to do. Once saved, there is no preparatory school, community college or military school to mature us as Christians. However, God does train us, perfect us and prepare us to fight our enemy. The word is our book of instruction and the Holy Spirit is our helper. In addition, God has equipped us with mighty weapons of warfare to fight and gain victory over our enemy. The testing/warfare help to mature us as Christians.

9 And I will put this third into the fire,
and refine them as one refines silver,
and test them as gold is tested.
They will call upon my name,
and I will answer them.
I will say, 'They are my people';
and they will say, 'The LORD is my God.'
Zechariah 13:9 (ESV)

Since our enemy strategically plans to defeat us by using all the knowledge he has gained regarding us through the use of familiar spirits, we must therefore use the weapons supplied to us by God to fight.

Spiritual Warfare Counsel - As given by the Apostle Paul

"For we wrestle not against flesh and blood, but against principalities, against powers, against the rulers of the darkness of this world, against spiritual wickedness in high places." Ephesians 6:12 (KJV)

("For the weapons of our warfare are not carnal, but mighty through God to the pulling down of stronghold ;") 2 Corinthians 10:4 (KJV)

- ✓ Use of these weapons of warfare are the means by which we achieve victory
- ✓ There is no single weapon alone that will defeat Satan
- ✓ Victory comes by putting on the armor of God and through proper use of one or more or all the weapons listed.

Weapons of Spiritual Warfare - As given by the Apostle Paul

Ephesians 6:14-17 (as noted below)

BELT OF TRUTH

The truth of God's word helps prevent us from living in error, deception and sin. It is the foundation used to support our weapons and ammunition.

SHOES OF THE GOSPEL OF PEACE

The peace of the gospel provides firm, unalterable footing as we proclaim the good news of salvation everywhere.

BREASTPLATE OF RIGHTEOUSNESS

Once we have been made the righteousness of God we should willingly live a holy life and be pleasing to God.

2 Cor. 5:21 says,...God put the wrong on him who never did anything wrong, so we could be put right with God. (MSG)

SHIELD OF FAITH

Faith must be used the same way shields are utilized in a battle. The Bible states, "the just shall live by faith".

Without it, it is impossible to please God.

HELMET OF SALVATION

The helmet protects our minds, the prime target of attack in all of our battles with Satan.

SWORD OF THE SPIRIT

The word of God is the most powerful weapon we can use against the enemy. The word cuts and exposes everything opposed to its life-giving principles.

ADDITIONAL WEAPONS OF SPIRITUAL WARFARE

PRAISE AND WORSHIP

A. PRAISE

1. *[6]Let the high praises of God be in their mouth, and a two-edged sword in their hand; [7] To execute vengeance upon the heathen, and punishments upon the people; [8] To bind their kings with chains, and their nobles with fetters of iron;[9] To execute upon them the judgment written: this honour have all his saints. Praise ye the LORD. Psalm 149:6-9 (KJV)*

2. *God is a Spirit: and they that worship him must worship him in spirit and in truth. John 4:24 (KJV)*

3. *But thou art holy, O thou that inhabitest the praises of Israel. Psalm 22:3 (KJV)*

B. CLAPPING

1. *'Thus says the Lord GOD: "Pound your fists and stamp your feet, and say, 'Alas, for all the evil abominations of the house of Israel! For they shall fall by the sword, by*

famine, and by pestilence. Ezekiel 6:11 (NKJV)

2. *Men shall clap their hands at him, and shall hiss him out of his place. Job 27:23 (NKJV)*

C. SHOUTING

1. *Joshua and his followers did a warfare "shout" and the walls of Jericho fell down. The warfare "shout" can and will put the devil to flight, so we can use the warfare "shout" to bring deliverance, healing, financial breakthrough and whatever else is needed. (see Joshua 6)*

2. *He makes my feet like the feet of a deer and set me secure on the heights. Psalm 18:33 (ESV)*

D. MUSIC

1. *16) Let the word of Christ dwell in you richly in all wisdom; teaching and admonishing one another in Psalms and hymns and spiritual songs, singing with grace in your hearts to the Lord. 17) And whatsoever ye do in word or deed, do all in the name of the Lord Jesus, giving thanks to God and the Father by him. Colossians 3:16-17 (KJV)*

2. *15) But now bring me a musician. Then it happened, when the musician played, that the hand of the LORD came upon him. 16) And he said, "Thus says the LORD: 'Make this valley full of ditches.' 17) For thus says the LORD: 'You shall not see wind, nor shall you see rain; yet that valley shall be filled with water, so that you, your cattle, and your animals may drink.' 18) And this is a simple matter in the sight of the LORD; He will also deliver the Moabites into your hand. 19) Also you shall attack every fortified city and every choice city, and shall cut down every good tree, and stop up every spring of water, and ruin every good piece of land with stones." 2 Kings 3:15-19 (NKJV)*

E. DANCING

1. *Warfare dance can bring deliverance to a city, church, family, or any situations as led by the Holy Spirit. Along with the use of banners, and flags, many of the dance, movements will include sharp kicks, jumps, leaps, stomping, marching, punching, pushing, and falling movements. Source: Dance Anointing Part II – Warfare dance, Victoria Ho*

2. *Let them praise His name with the dance; Let them sing praises to Him with the timbrel and harp. Psalm 149:3 (NKJV)*

F. STOMPING & MARCHING

1. *Thus says the Lord God: "Pound your fists and stamp your feet and say, 'Alas, for all the evil abominations of the house of Israel! For they shall fall by the sword, by famine, and by pestilence. Ezekiel 6:1 (NKJV), (see Joshua 6)*

FAITH

A. SHIELD OF FAITH

(Repeated again.) The shield of faith is used in spiritual battle. It is a defensive weapon used to protect the soldier from the fiery darts thrown by Satan and his demons. Historically, soldiers wore shields over their chest to prevent the penetration of arrows and swords into their bodies. Faith is the weapon used to protect our soul and preserve our spiritual life, thus, preventing spiritual death, which results from the wounds inflicted by the enemy.

Jesus answered and said unto them, Verily I say unto you, If ye have faith, and doubt not, ye shall not only do this which is done to the fig tree, but also if ye shall say unto this mountain, Be thou removed, and be thou cast into the sea; it shall be done.
Matthew 21:21(KJV)

And Jesus answering saith unto them, Have faith in God. Mark 11:22 (KJV)

THE BLOOD OF THE LAMB

They overcame him by the blood of the Lamb, and by the word of their testimony;...Revelation 12:11 (KJV)

PRAYER

A. PRAYING

Now when Solomon had made an end of praying, the fire came down from heaven, and consumed the burnt offering and the sacrifices; and the glory of the Lord filled the house. 2 Chronicles 7:1 (KJV)

B. PRAYING IN THE SPIRIT

Praying always with all prayer and supplication in the Spirit, watching thereunto with all perseverance and supplication for all saints; Ephesians 6:18 (KJV)

FASTING

"And he said to them, This kind can come forth by nothing, but by prayer and fasting." Mark 9:29 (KJV)

Is not this the fast that I have chosen? to loose the bands of wickedness, to undo the heavy burdens, and to let the oppressed go free, and that ye break every yoke? Isaiah 58:6 (KJV)

THE NAME OF JESUS

"That at the name of Jesus every knee should bow, of things in heaven, and things in earth, and things under the earth;" Philippians 2:10 (KJV)

THE WORD OF GOD

"For the word of God is quick, and powerful, and sharper than any two-edged sword, piercing even to the dividing asunder of soul and spirit, and of the joints and marrow, and is a discerner of the thoughts and intents of the heart." Hebrews 4:12 (KJV)

ANGELS

" Bless the LORD, ye his angels that excel in strength, that do his commandments, hearkening unto the voice of his word." Psalm 103:20 (KJV)

"For he shall give his angels charge over thee, to keep thee in all thy ways."
Psalm 91:11(KJV)

"Are they not all ministering spirits, sent forth to minister for them who shall be heirs of salvation?" Hebrews 1:14 (KJV)

MONEY

A. **TITHING AND SOWING OFFERINGS IS USED TO DISSEMINATE THE GOSPEL**
"For wisdom is a defense as money is a defense, But the excellence of knowledge is that wisdom gives life to those who have it." Ecclesiastes 7:12 (KJV)
Source: Rules of Engagement, Cindy Trim, Charisma House, 2008

"A feast is made for laughter, And wine makes merry; But money answers everything." Ecclesiastes 10:19 (KJV)

11) "You ask, 'How have we robbed you?'

"The tithe and the offering—that's how! And now you're under a curse—the whole lot of you—because you're robbing me. Bring your full tithe to the Temple treasury so there will be ample provisions in my Temple. Test me in this and see if I don't open up heaven itself to you and pour out blessings beyond your wildest dreams. For my part, I will defend you against marauders, protect your wheat fields and vegetable gardens against

plunderers." The Message of GOD-of-the-Angel-Armies.

12) "You'll be voted 'Happiest Nation.' You'll experience what it's like to be a country of grace." GOD-of-the-Angel-Armies says so. Malachi 3:10-12

LAUGHTER

1) Laughter is an antidote to pain, stress and depression.
2) Laughter naturally produces endorphins in the body, which help strengthen your immune system, increase bodily energy and produce relaxation.
3) Laughter is a weapon.

GIFTS OF THE SPIRIT

I Corinthians 12: 8-10
(Specifically the Discernment of Spirit, Word of Knowledge and Prophetic)

A. **DISCERNMENT**
Discernment is a supernatural ability given by the Holy Spirit to determine whether a spiritual manifestation is good or evil, of God or of Satan.

16) "And it came to pass, as we went to prayer, a certain damsel possessed with a spirit of divination met us, which brought her masters much gain by soothsaying: 17) The same followed Paul and us, and cried, saying, These men are the servants of the most high God, which shew unto us the way of salvation. 18) And this did she many days. But Paul, being grieved, turned and said to the spirit, I command thee in the name of Jesus Christ to come out of her. And he came out the same hour." Acts 16:16-18 (KJV)

18) "And when Simon saw that through laying on of the apostles' hands the Holy Ghost was given, he offered them money, 19)Saying, Give me also this power, that on whomsoever I lay hands, he may receive the Holy Ghost. 20) But Peter said unto him, Thy money perish with thee, because thou hast thought that the gift of God may be purchased with money. 21) Thou hast neither part nor lot in this matter: for thy heart is not right in the sight of God. 22) Repent therefore of this thy wickedness, and pray God, if perhaps the thought of thine heart may be forgiven thee. 23) For I perceive that thou art in the gall of bitterness, and in the bond of iniquity." Acts 8:18-23 (KJV)

B. WISDOM

Wisdom is the insight and understanding to know the will and thinking of God on a matter and to apply it.

"Wisdom is better than weapons of war;" Ecclesiastes 9:18a (KJV)

C. PROPHETIC ANOINTING

The prophetic anointing for purposes of this study shall be defined as men and women anointed to hear, speak and declare what they have heard from God concerning a person, place or thing.

5) "And if anyone wants to harm them, fire proceeds from their mouth and devours their enemies. And if anyone wants to harm them, he must be killed in this manner. 6) These have power to shut heaven, so that no rain falls in the days of their prophecy; and they have power over waters to turn them to blood, and to strike the earth with all plagues, as often as they desire." Revelation 11:5-6 (NKJV)

OTHER SPIRITUALS GIFTS INCLUDE:

1) **HEALING** – The miraculous power of God to restore spiritual, physical and emotional health.
2) **MIRACLES** – The visual manifestation of signs and wonders.

3) **HELPS** – Doing whatever it takes to accomplish a task needed for kingdom ministry.
4) **TONGUES/INTERPRETATION OF TONGUES** – The communication of God to men and the interpretation of what is being said from God to men. It can also be the ability to speak in foreign language with no prior learning.
5) **FAITH** – Supernatural faith in God to do something.

POWER

A. AUTHORITY

"Behold I give unto you power to tread on serpents and scorpions, and over all the power of the enemy: and nothing shall by any means hurt you." Luke 10:19 (KJV)

B. BINDING AND LOOSING

God gives us the keys to the kingdom so we can bind the powers of darkness and loose the things of God. Matthew 16:19 (KJV) (see Matthew 12:28-29)

C. LAYING ON OF HANDS

Performed when men were promoted into leadership, and in baptism and receiving of the Holy Ghost.

" And when Paul had laid his hands upon them, the Holy Ghost came on them; and they spake with tongues, and prophesied." Acts 19:6 (KJV)

"Lay hands suddenly on no man, neither be partaker of other men's sins: keep thyself pure." I Timothy 5:22 (KJV)

D. ANOINTING WITH OIL

Usually signifies that something is sacred, to consecrate or to set apart, and dedicate for its attention and use unto God

"And they cast out many devils, and anointed with oil many that were sick, and healed them." Mark 6:13 (KJV)

"...That his burden will be taken away from your shoulder, And his yoke from your neck, And the yoke will be destroyed because of the anointing oil." Isaiah 10:27(NKJV)

OTHER

WARFARE - A WAR OF WORDS

"Spiritual warfare is a war of words. Spiritual warfare is a war of the mind". Your words represent the thoughts in the mind (ideas). The thoughts in the mind represent the state of one's heart (feelings, emotions). In other words, as a person goes through warfare, the speech that exits their mouth will either convey victory, defeat, faith or failure. Words will either represent positive decrees and declarations or negative proclamations, which agree with the enemy.

"We must legislate, like David did in 1 Samuel chapter 17, with our words". While I recommend you read the entire chapter, please focus on the words of David from the scriptures below. This is only one scriptural example of how to warfare with words. *Source: Bishop West Obiakaraue of Aba, Nigeria*

26)... Who does he think he is, anyway, this uncircumcised Philistine, taunting the armies of God - Alive?" (MSG)

34-37) David said, "I've been a shepherd, tending sheep for my father. Whenever a lion or bear came and took a lamb from the flock, I'd go after it, knock it down, and rescue the lamb. If it turned on me, I'd grab it by the throat, wring its neck, and kill it. Lion or bear, it made no difference — I killed it. And I'll do the same to this Philistine pig who is taunting the troops of God-Alive. GOD, who delivered me from the teeth of the lion and the claws of the bear, will deliver me from this Philistine."

45-47) David answered, "You come at me with sword and spear and battle-ax. I come at you in the name of GOD-of-the-Angel-Armies, the God of Israel's troops, whom you curse and mock. This very day GOD is handing you over to me. I'm about to kill you, cut off your head, and serve up your body and the bodies of your Philistine buddies to the crows and coyotes. The whole earth will know that there's an extraordinary God in Israel. And everyone gathered here will learn that GOD doesn't save by means of sword or spear. The battle belongs to GOD — he's handing you to us on a platter!"(MSG)

Other than our body language, words may very well be the most commonly used method to translate our position in a spiritual conflict. Always be careful to guard your words and make sure they are words that will win the war.

CHAPTER 3

The Hierarchy of the Two Kingdoms

For by him all things were created that are in heaven and that are on earth, visible and invisible, whether thrones or dominions or principalities or powers. All things were created through him and for him. *Colossians 1:16 (KJV)*

The Hierarchy of the Two Kingdoms

THE HIERARCHY OF GOD'S KINGDOM

SERAPHIM/CHERUBIM

Seraphim worship God continually and

are closest to the throne of God.

They cry "Holy, Holy, is the Lord of Hosts!"

Cherubim guard the throne of God.

GOD'S HIGH RANK ANGELS

First in rank and first in political power among the angels

1) Michael the Chief Prince means "who is like God" or "God is my strength". He is chief warrior angel.
2) Gabriel means "strong man of God". He is a messenger angel.

Source: ww.christcenteredmall.com/teachings/angels

Other Classes of Angels

Thrones, Dominions, Principalities
Authorities and Powers in Heavenly Places
(Over world systems, and nations)
(Colossians 1:16; Ephesians 3:10; 1:20 – 21; 1 Peter 3:22)

ANGELS – *God's kingdom includes angelic beings called angels.*

Angels are spiritual beings created by God

The Angels of God are innumerable

Psalms 68:17, Revelation 5:11

Angels are both visible and invisible

Be not forgetful to entertain strangers: for thereby some have entertained angels unawares. Hebrews 13:2 (KJV)

Angels act within the sovereign authority of God

Satan and his demons also act within the sovereign authority of God.

An angel's primary function is to serve God and minister to human beings

They deliver God's messages and bring comfort and protection to God's people. (Psalms 91:11, Matthew 4:6, Mark 1:13)

Are not all angels ministering spirits sent to serve those who will be heirs of salvation? Hebrews 1:14 (NKJV)

Angels engage in continual spiritual warfare

This warfare is conducted on both the macro and micro level. In other words, this warfare concerns the affairs of governments and individuals.

Bless the LORD, ye his angels that excel in strength, that do his commandments, hearkening unto the voice of his word. Psalms 103:20

Most holy angels are referred to as the very elect of God (*1Timothy 5:21)*

"The bible doesn't make a big deal regarding the activity of angels. Our focus should be on Jesus Christ, to whom all creation - even angels - will one day bow down".

Source: "What Does the Bible Say About" from Thomas Nelson Publishers (2001)

THE HIERARCHY OF SATAN'S KINGDOM

PRINCIPALITIES - Influences National Policies and World Leaders

POWERS – Affects Five Systems: Society, Marriage, Government, Education and Church

RULERS OF THE DARKNESS – Blinds the Mind of the People to the Truth and Salvation

SPIRITUAL WICKNESS IN HIGH PLACES – Prevents Answers to Prayer and Perverts

DEMONS

When Satan rose up against God, he was kicked out of heaven and a third of the angels rebelled and was kicked out with him. Those rebellious angels are satanic spirits known as demons.

Demons Have Personality Attributes

Will - *Then he saith, I will return into my house from whence I came out; and when he is come, he findeth it empty, swept, and garnished. Matthew 12:44 (KJV)*

Intellect – 23) *And there was in their synagogue a man with an unclean spirit; and he cried out,*
24) Saying, Let us alone; what have we to do with thee, thou Jesus of Nazareth? art thou come to destroy us? I know thee who thou art, the Holy One of God. Mark 1:23-24 (KJV)

Emotions - *Thou believest that there is one God; thou doest well: the devils also believe, and tremble. James 2:19 (KJV)*

Self-Awareness - *And he asked him, What is thy name? And he answered, saying, My name is Legion: for we are many. Mark 5:9 (KJV)*

Nature of Demons or Satanic Spirits

- ✓ Demons are not humans but they do seek to dwell in humans.
- ✓ They are evil and oppose everything and everyone associated with God.
- ✓ They are supernatural thinkers, quick and intelligent.
- ✓ They have knowledge of an individual's generational history, addictions, traits, illnesses, etc. They seek to influence and control an individual's future.
- ✓ They have personalities but more importantly, they seek to influence the personality of the individual they inhabit.
- ✓ They are very powerful but their power is limited by the saint who chooses to operate in the authority that has been given to them by God.

Demons

Seek to influence the sphere of communication

Demons

Talk, congregate and fellowship

Demons

Preach doctrines and work miracles

ADDITIONAL ATTRIBUTES OF DEMONIC/SATANIC SPIRITS

- ✓ The ability to speak *(Mark 1:24)*
- ✓ Entice, tempt *(James 1:14; I Thess. 3:5)*
- ✓ Deceive *(I Tim 4:1)*
- ✓ Torment *(II Timothy 1:7; I John 4:18; Matthew 18:33-34)*
- ✓ Drive (compel, compulsive) *(Luke 8:29)*
- ✓ Defile (*Mark 5:15)*
- ✓ Fight against peace *(Matthew 12:43-45)*
- ✓ Attack our physical well-being *(Luke 13:11-16)*

- ✓ Resist and oppose *(Matthew 13:19; II Cor. 4:4; Zech. 3:1-3)*
- ✓ Pervert the word and seek to hinder the gospel *(I Thess. 2:18)*
- ✓ Blind the minds of believers *(II Cor. 4:4)*
- ✓ Hold people captive *(II Tim. 3:7)*
- ✓ Seduce people, lead people astray *(I Tim. 4:1; Mark 13:22; I John 2:26)*
- ✓ Trouble people (make them fearful, afraid, terrify them) *(I Sam.16:14; I Chron. 10:13-14)*
- ✓ Oppress, Enslave people *(Romans 8:15; Acts 10:38)*
- ✓ Vex people (cause painful feelings, passions and sufferings, to harass) *(Matthew 15:22; 17:15; Luke 6:18; Acts 5:18)*
- ✓ Possess people (occupy and own a person; indwell and control) (Mark 1:23-24)
- ✓ Invade our thoughts *(II Cor. 10:3-5; Matthew 4:1-11)*

Source: Based on the teachings of Derek Prince, They shall Expel Demons, Chosen Books Angel Bible study, Christian Teaching on Angel and christcenteredmall.com

THREE CATEGORIES OF DEMONS:

I. Territorial Spirits

- ✓ "Territorial Spirits" is used to describe a demonic occupation of a specific geographical location

- ✓ The following passages imply that fallen angels have been given assignments over certain geographical areas and are said to have a territorial presence in a specific area. Individuals who are attuned to the spiritual realm and enter another city, town, or country can readily notice a change in the atmosphere. Immediately or over time, the Holy Spirit will begin to identify the strongman, their cohorts and the familiar spirits that operate in a specific territory.

- ✓ Demons are definitely at work in the spiritual realm and believers are very much involved in a battle against them

  Daniel 10; John 12:31; John 14:30; John 16:11; Mark 5:10 and Ephesians 6:12.
  Source: Angels: Elect & Evil by C. Fred Dickason

TERRITORIES/FOUR WORLD DIVISION

FIRST WORLD	**Europe, North America, Japan, South Africa, and secular Israel**
SECOND WORLD	**Middle East Arabic states, Russia, Eastern Europe, former Soviet Union, Turkey, Armenia, Afghanistan**
Third World	**China, Northern Africa, South American, Brazil, Venezuela, and Argentina, Mexico, Central America, Southeast Asia**
Fourth World	**Ethiopia/ Eritrea, Sub-Saharan Africa, parts of Asia-Mongolia, Nepal, Tibet**

Source: nationonline.org, quickreferenceforall.org and wiki.answers.com

The next two (2) maps show the people (nationality), economics and the spirituality of a territory.

(If manual is printed in color refer to legend.
If manual is printed in black and white, refer to maps online for greater detail).

MAP #1- People Group Status Map
Legend: THE FOUR WORLD MODEL MAP

Royal Blue	1st World
Red	Second World
Lime Green	Third World
Dark Green	Fourth World

MAP #2 - Progress of the Gospel by People Group
Legend: PROGRESS OF THE GOSPEL BY PEOPLE GROUP
Based on the Joshua Progress Scale April 2014

Gray	Data not available or inhibited
Green	Established/Significant
Yellow	Formative/Nominal
Red	Unreached/Least Reached

Source: THE FOUR WORLD MODEL MAP

Wikipedia.com

Territories may be defined geographically by continent, state, city, county, and township or even broken down directionally, historically, economically and politically.

Progress of the Gospel by People Group
Based on the Joshua Project Progress Scale
People Group Status
Data not available or uninhabited
Established / Significant
Formative / Nominal
Unreached / Least-Reached
Source: Joshua Project (www.joshuaproject.net), April 2014
Map by Joshua Project and Global Mapping International (www.gmi.org)

II. Familiar Spirits

The term familiar spirits refers to the practice of talking or consulting with the dead. Familiar spirits are used by mediums or psychics, necromancers, charmers, fortunetellers, etc. to inquire, call upon, consult the dead, or seek direction or answers to questions from the dead. Some Biblical scholars only used this definition to refer to one consulting the dead. However, many deliverance ministers, including myself, associate the activities of these spirits as being more than just spirits of the dead conversing with the living. The term familiar spirits also refers to spirits that are intimately acquainted and unduly personal with an individual, family or generational line (family or familiar). These spirits are specifically assigned to individuals and serve as spirit companions. They know all about the individual, their family issues, generational characteristics, etc. They serve, prompt or induce individuals to action. They can be present in our homes and with us without the use of a medium, etc.

God strictly forbade this heathen practice among the Israelites *(Leviticus 19:31, Acts 16:16, I Samuel 28:8, 11-14, Deuteronomy 18:10-13)*

- ✓ Saul, the first King of Israel tried it *(1 Samuel 28:3-25)*. He went to a sorcerer to call up the dead prophet Samuel for some urgent advice. Sure enough, Samuel appeared, though it was a demon spirit.

- ✓ The Bible is very clear the dead have nothing to do with the living. "For the living know that they shall die but the dead know not anything, neither have they any more a reward; for the memory of them is forgotten." *Ecclesiastes 9:5 (KJV)*

III. Seducing Spirits

Seducing spirits are responsible for attracting and drawing you into a wrong or foolish course of action. The enemy uses the three gates to your soul/flesh to seduce an individual. Those 3 gates are described in *1 John 2:16 (KJV);*

[16] For all that is in the world, the lust of the flesh, and the lust of the eyes, and the pride of life, is not of the Father, but is of the world. They are:

1. Lust of the Flesh
2. Lust of the Eyes
3. Pride of Life

CHAPTER 4

WHERE WARFARE BEGINS

- In the Mind

For God has not given us a spirit of fear,
But of power, and of love, and of a sound mind.
2 Timothy 1:7 (KJV)

Where Warfare Begins – In the Mind

What is the Mind and why is it so important?
The mind is best described by the Greek word "nous" or "dianoia". It is used to describe the mental functions of perceptions, thoughts, understanding and intellect. It is the place where a man's reasoning, conscience and imagination reside.

What does Satan want with your mind?
Satan wants to enter into the mind of the believer, take over his thoughts, control his desires and temptations; thus, influencing him/her to yield their will in opposition to the will of God. Satan wants your mind to influence you to sin against God.

The thief cometh not, but for to steal, and to kill, and to destroy: ... John 10:10 (KJV)

Satan conveys a thought to your mind and offer suggestions thru one or more of the (3) gates:

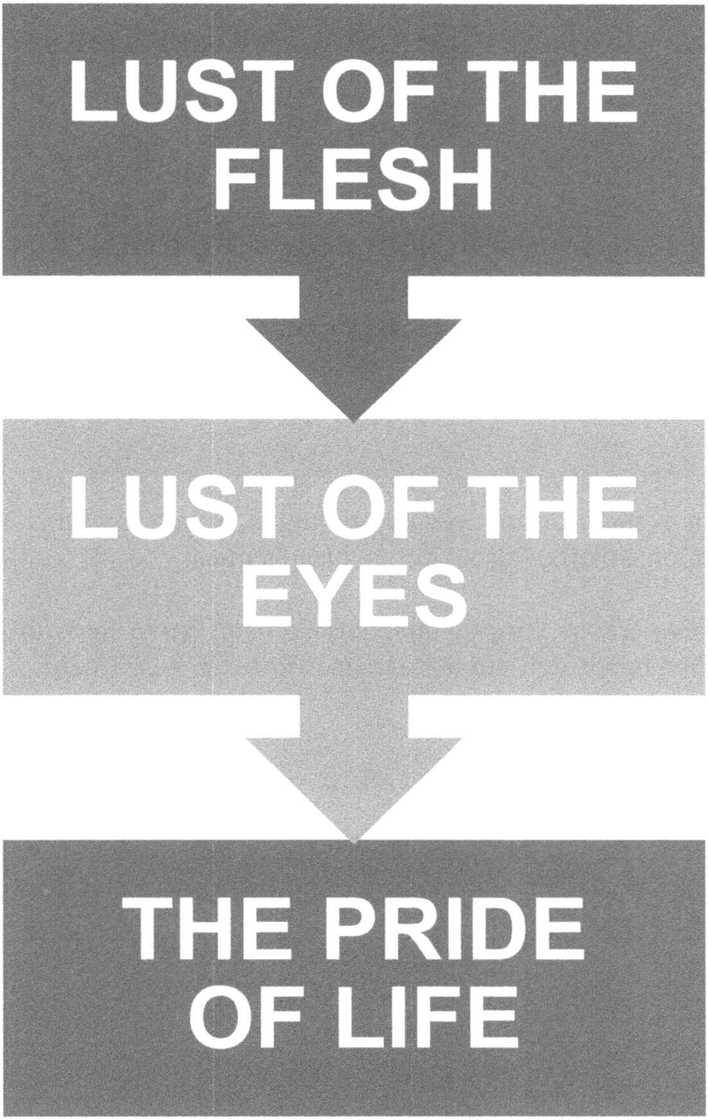

LUST OF THE FLESH

↓

LUST OF THE EYES

↓

THE PRIDE OF LIFE

For all that is in the world - the lust of the flesh, the lust of the eyes, and the pride of life - is not of the Father but is of the world. 1 John 2:16 (NKJV)

OR...

Nothing in the world comes from the Father.
I mean the wrong things people like to do with their bodies.
I mean the things people see and want to have. I mean all the things people are proud of in this life. These things come from the world, not the Father. 1 John 2:16 (New Testament) (WE)

For out of the heart proceed evil thoughts, murders, adulteries, fornications, thefts, false witness, blasphemies:

20) These are the things which defile a man: but to eat with unwashen hands defileth not a man. *Matt 15:19-20 (KJV)*

OR...

Here is what comes from the heart:
wrong thoughts, killing people,
all kinds of adultery, stealing, lying,
and saying wrong things about people.
20These things make a person dirty.
To eat with hands that are not washed
does not make him dirty.' Matt 15:19-20 (WE)

PASSIVE MINDS ARE EASY TARGETS FOR THE ENEMY

Christians cannot afford to have spiritually inactive minds. Christians who do not renew their minds, with the word of God, can become spiritually neutral and their minds become open to invasion by the opposing force.

And the peace of God, which surpasses all understanding, will guard your hearts and your minds in Christ Jesus. Philippians 4:7 (ESV)

Christians must cast out negative thoughts from their minds and shut the enemy down. We must exercise our power and authority to resist Satan's attack. Christians must constantly renew their minds with the word of God. Praying the word of God renders a grand slam every time.

11-14) Get the word out. Teach all these things. And don't let anyone put you down because you're young. Teach believers with your life: by word, by demeanor, by love, by faith, by integrity. Stay at your post reading Scripture, giving counsel, teaching. And that special gift of ministry you were given when the leaders of the church laid hands on you and prayed - keep that dusted off and in use. 1Timothy 4:11-14 (MSG)

Spiritual Failure	Career Failure	Financial Failure
Bereavement	Disappointment	Marital Trouble
Family Issues	Idle Time	Health Issues
Unforgiveness	Abuse	Hatred

HOW DOES THE BATTLE START IN THE MIND?

This battle may start with a circumstance, happening or just an infiltration of thoughts. These circumstances or happenings could include situations such as the above:

Satan will utilize every tactic he can against your mind. His major attack will always come when you are most vulnerable. He will oppose you and be your chief adversary.

"Be sober, be vigilant; because your adversary the devil, as a roaring lion, walketh about, seeking whom he may devour." 1 Peter 5:8 (KJV)

Satan Desires To

- ✓ Oppose you in your mind because he's your Adversary
- ✓ Sow deception because he is the Father of Lies
- ✓ Deceive you in your mind because he is the Deceiver
- ✓ Tempt you in your mind because he is the Tempter, Liar and #1 Seducer
- ✓ Torment you in your mind because he wants to immobilize Christians until they are unable to walk in the victory and the power that God has planned and purposed
- ✓ Satan wants Christians to turn from the truth, from hearing and believing God's word

Satan Wants Us in a State of Spiritual Darkness so We Can Become

- ✓ We become alienated from God, His word
- ✓ We become isolated from fellowship with other saints of God
- ✓ We are unable and unwilling to hear God's voice
- ✓ We are disobedient
- ✓ We are unrepentant

THE RESULTS OF ALLOWING SATAN TO WIN THE BATTLE IN YOUR MIND

Depression:

Clinical depression affects 1 out of 20 individuals each month and is the leading cause of suicide - 10th leading cause of death. By the year 2020, depression will be the second most common health problem in the world.

Source: *PBS/Depression – Out of the Shadows*

Stress:

Physical, mental, or emotional strain or tension - affects the heart, lungs, mouth, muscles, brain, hair, digestive tract, skin and reproductive organs.

Worry:

To feel anxious; to torment oneself with or suffer from disturbing thoughts; to fret

Temptation:

The act of alluring, enticing

Hardened Hearts:

Rebellious, unforgiving and vengeful

Sin:

Demonstration of unbelief and participation in activities opposing the divine principles of God

THERE WERE TWO THAT REFUSED TO BE STRESSED

20) And brought them to the magistrates, saying, These men, being Jews, do exceedingly trouble our city,
21) And teach customs, which are not lawful for us to receive, neither to observe, being Romans. 22) And the multitude rose up together against them: and the

magistrates rent off their clothes, and commanded to beat them. 23) And when they had laid many stripes upon them, they cast them into prison, charging the jailor to keep them safely: 24) Who, having received such a charge, thrust them into the inner prison, and made their feet fast in the stocks. 25) And at midnight Paul and Silas prayed, and sang praises unto God: and the prisoners heard them. 26) And suddenly there was a great earthquake, so that the foundations of the prison were shaken: and immediately all the doors were opened, and every one's bands were loosed. Acts 16:20-26 (KJV)

BATTLE FOUGHT IN THE MIND MUST BE WON IN THE SPIRIT FIRST

Satan's ultimate objective is to "wear us down" in the area of our minds. He is constantly bombarding us with the worries of our past, what doesn't look good in our present and the possibilities of future happenings. He is constantly reminding us of our past and telling us what we cannot be. Satan wants an individual to deteriorate (become inferior in character, quality and value) to the point that they become ineffective, literally cannot function in life and even succumb to death. Therefore, it is important that we fight the battle of our mind in the spirit. As Satan keeps pressing us to dwell on one or more negative thoughts over and over again, we must always consume ourselves with the word of God, with our praise (spiritual songs), praying in spirit with prophetic utterance yielding fatal blows to every attack the enemy throws at us. Remember that victory in the mind cannot be won with physical blows and punches.

Source: Morris Cerullo, Winning the Battle for your Mind, Volume 3

The weapons we fight with are not the weapons of the world. On the contrary, they have divine power to demolish strongholds. 2 Corinthians 10:4 (NIV)

HOW TO WIN THE BATTLE IN THE MIND

1. **We win by refusing to give Satan access to our mind.**

   Therefore submit to God. Resist the devil and he will flee from you. James 4:7 (NKJV)

2. **We win by recognizing God's voice as opposed to Satan's. Satan will always attempt to convince you to oppose the word of God, often using a partial truth to convince you.**

   3) To him the porter openeth; and the sheep hear his voice: and he calleth his own sheep by name, and leadeth them out. 4) And when he putteth forth his own sheep, he goeth before them, and the sheep follow him: for they know his voice. 5) And a stranger will they not follow, but will flee from him: for they know not the voice of strangers. John 10:3-5 (KJV)

3. **Cleanse your mind.**

And do not be conformed to this world, but be transformed by the renewing of your mind, that you may prove what is that good and acceptable and perfect will of God. Romans 12:2 (NKJV)

4. **Pull down strongholds and renew your mind with the word of God.**

   4) For the weapons of our warfare are not carnal, but mighty through God to the pulling down of strong holds; 5) Casting down imaginations, and every high thing that exalteth itself against the knowledge of God, and bringing into captivity every thought to the obedience of Christ; 2 Corinthians 10:4-5 (KJV)

5. **Increase your faith by praying in the Holy Ghost.**

   But ye, beloved, building up yourselves on your most holy faith, praying in the Holy Ghost. Jude 1:20 (KJV)

6. **Identify and test the spirits attacking your mind. Recognize the one spirit that always shows up; the spirit of fear. You must Pull Down Fear!**

Pull Down

fear of death, fear of failure, fear of persecution, peer pressure
fear of calamity, fear of hunger, fear of sickness, fear of danger
fear of Satan and his demons, etc.

"Beloved, do not believe every spirit, but test the spirits to see whether they are from God, because many false prophets have gone out into the world." 1 John 4 (NASB)

"For God hath not given us the spirit of fear; but of power, and of love, and of a sound mind."
2 Timothy 1:7 (KJV)

7. **Declare the promises of God and speak them out of your mouth.**

For all the promises of God in him are yea, and in him Amen, unto the glory of God by us.
2 Corinthians 1:20 (KJV)

Let the redeemed of the LORD say so, whom he hath redeemed from the hand of the enemy; Psalm 107:2 (KJV)

8. **<u>Get spiritually violent and use your spiritual weapons</u>**

And from the days of John the Baptist until now the kingdom of heaven suffereth violence,
and the violent take it by force. Matthew 11:12 (KJV)

9. **<u>Pray, praise and worship God daily</u>**

And he shall live, and to him shall be given of the gold of Hebrews: prayer also shall be made for him continually; and daily shall he be praised. Psalm 72:15 (KJV)

Blessed be the Lord, who daily loadeth us with benefits, even the God of our salvation. Selah. Psalm 68:19 (KJV)

God is a Spirit: and they that worship him must worship him in spirit and in truth. John 4:24 (KJV)

Rejoice in the LORD, O ye righteous: for praise is comely for the upright. Psalm 33:1(KJV)

Source: Based on Morris Cerullo, Exposing Satan's Strategies, Volume 4

CHAPTER 5

Deliverance - Freeing the Captive

I've tried everything and nothing helps. I'm at the end of my rope. Is there no one who can do anything for me? Isn't that the real question? The answer, thank God, is that Jesus Christ can and does. He acted to set things right in this life of contradictions where I want to serve God with all my heart and mind, but am pulled by the influence of sin to do something totally different.
Romans 7:24-25 (MSG)

Deliverance - Freeing the Captive

What is Deliverance?

Deliverance is a method, established by God, to remove the effects of demonic influence. These influences are ushered in through our varied backgrounds and experiences including social, economic, and educational surroundings. Deliverance closes the doors to the soul both before and after you come to know Christ as Lord and Savior. These open doors are used to hinder spiritual growth, rob you of your peace and diminish your joy. They can kill your success and destroy your chance to fulfill the destiny God has for your life.

God's plan for our life is that we have peace, joy and success. It is Satan's plan to steal our peace, joy and success. No matter what we go through in life, deliverance is one method, provided by God to help us regain peace, joy and success. Even if we find ourselves lacking in the areas of peace, joy and success we can be confident that we can always get them back again.

- ✓ We can obtain peace which is unexplainable (Philippians 4:7)
- ✓ We can have that joy, not based on circumstances and happenings (1Peter 1:8); because it is God who gives real joy and we can also have success (Joshua 1:8)
- ✓ We can be profitable, forever producing for ourselves and for the kingdom of God

All of these kingdom benefits cannot be accomplished until we are free from demonic oppression. God has given us the ministry of deliverance to help us enjoy all the benefits of the kingdom. Yet, it is God's intention that as we warfare, we warfare well; hence, the need for the deliverance ministry.

DELIVERANCE BRINGS

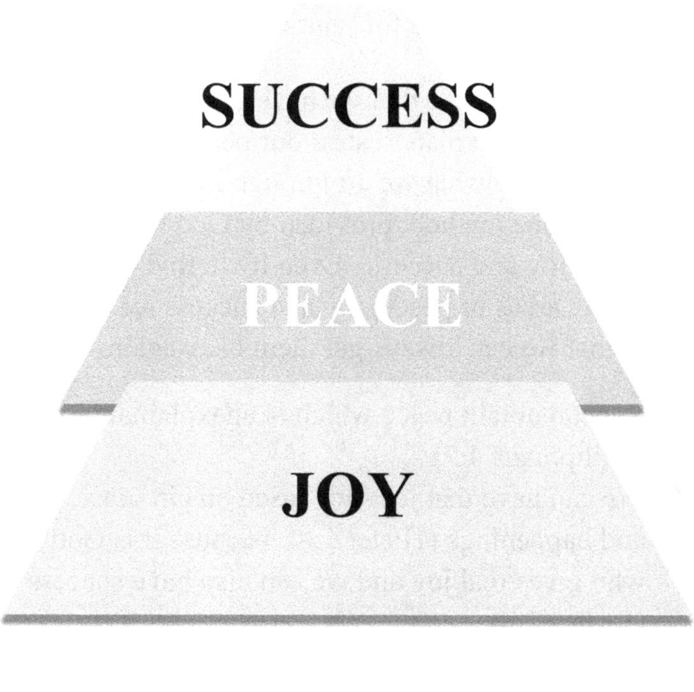

SUCCESS

PEACE

JOY

4) Surely he hath borne our griefs, and carried our sorrows: 5) But he was wounded for our transgressions, he was bruised for our iniquities: the chastisement of our peace was upon him; and with his stripes we are healed. Isaiah 53:4-5(KJV)

Deliverance means to be *rescued* or brought back from something *evil*, demonic; *restored and saved* (www.merriam-webster.com). The word deliverance comes from the Greek word *sozo*, which stands for salvation, meaning to save, do well and be whole (www.biblestudytools.com). The ministry of deliverance is aimed at assisting our brothers and sisters in walking in the liberty, achieved by Christ, when he died and rose from the grave.

When you make Christ the Lord of your life, your spirit is new but your body and mind (soul) remain the same. Your mind becomes renewed/changed over time, with the word of God, but should this area go unattended, in lack of the word of God, the devil will gain access to the mind and continue to influence you in sin. The Holy Spirit can be grieved and quenched when there is sin in the life of the believer; therefore, we must be quick to repent. Depending on the type of sin or bondage you participated in, you may need to be delivered.

Who Is Deliverance For?

The Bible tells us that Deliverance is "the children's bread" and that it should be used for the children. Just as bread is a major staple of our diet, deliverance has always been considered a major part of the Christians' diet.

Most Christians partake of their diet at their local church. Just like the preaching of the word, prayer and worship are a part of the local church experience. The deliverance ministry must also be a major ministry in the local church and seen as a normal function of ministry. Thus, if deliverance is not a major function of the local church ministry, then the children will not get filled. Just as bread helps fill the nutritional gaps in the diet and helps us feel full and satisfied, the ministry of deliverance, when made available to the believer, provides necessary spiritual, nutrition and contentment.

26) The woman was a Greek, a Syro -Phoenician by birth, and she kept asking Him to cast the demon out of her daughter. 27) But Jesus said to her, "Let the children be filled first, for it is not good to take the children's bread and throw it to the little dogs." Mark 7:26-27 (NKJV)

Jesus Healed All Who were oppressed by the Devil *(Acts 10:38)*

Jesus performed deliverances everywhere he went. Subsequently, his disciples cast out demons everywhere they went.

Jesus, undeterred, went right ahead
and gave his charge:
"God authorized and commanded me
to commission you:
Go out and train everyone you meet, far and near, in this way of life, marking them by baptism in the threefold name: Father, Son, and Holy Spirit.

Then instruct them in the practice
of all I have commanded you.
I'll be with you as you do this, day after day after day, right up to the end of the age." *Matthew 28:18-20 (MSG)*

Christians are to observe the same things that Jesus taught the disciples.

Tell them that the kingdom is here.
Bring health to the sick.
Raise the dead. Touch the untouchables.
Kick out the demons.
You have been treated generously, so live generously.
Matthew 10:7-8 (MSG)

"These are some of the signs that
will accompany believers:
They will throw out demons in my name, they will speak in new tongues, they will take snakes in their hands, they will drink poison and not be

hurt, they will lay hands on the sick and make them well." Mark 16:17-18 (MSG)

Jesus sent his twelve harvest hands out with this charge:

"Don't begin by traveling to some far-off
place to convert unbelievers.
And don't try to be dramatic by tackling
some public enemy.
Go to the lost, confused people right
here in the neighborhood.
Tell them that the kingdom is here.
Bring health to the sick.
Raise the dead. Touch the untouchables.
Kick out the demons.
You have been treated generously,
so live generously"
Matt. 10:5 (MSG)

According to scriptures, if we believe on Christ, we shall do the greater works.

"Verily, *verily, I say unto you, He that believeth on me, the works that I do shall he do also; and greater works than these shall he do; because I go unto my Father". John 14:12 (KJV)*

Deliverance can be ministered through prayer, confession and faith in the word of God. It can also be ministered through counseling and the casting out of demons. Deliverance is the portal by which we can become truly free from bondage, vices, broken-heartedness and sickness as we are transformed into the absolute likeness of Christ.

The ministry of deliverance, comprised over half the New Testament ministry of Jesus. The reason for deliverance is clearly affirmed in Isaiah 61:1-3 and reaffirmed in Luke 4:18. The ministry of Jesus was not just for the chosen Jews but Jesus died for the sins of the entire world, Hallelujah! Thus, Jesus came so that captives could be set free, the bound could be released from their bondage and those with broken hearts could be healed. He came to do the Father's business, which includes the delivery of glad tidings, resulting in salvation and deliverance for all.

1) The Spirit of the Lord GOD is upon me; because the LORD hath anointed me to preach good tidings unto the meek; he hath sent me to bind up the brokenhearted, to proclaim liberty to the captives, and the opening of the prison to them that are bound;

2) To proclaim the acceptable year of the LORD, and the day of vengeance of our God; to comfort all that mourn; 3) To appoint unto them that mourn in Zion, to give unto them beauty for ashes, the oil of joy for mourning, the garment of praise for the spirit of heaviness; that they might be called trees of righteousness, the planting of the LORD, that he might be glorified. Isaiah 61:1-3 (KJV)

18 The Spirit of the Lord is upon me,
because he hath anointed me to preach
the gospel to the poor;
he hath sent me to heal the brokenhearted,
to preach deliverance to the captives,
and recovering of sight to the blind,
to set at liberty them that are bruised,
Luke 4:18 (KJV)

Deliverance is available for all who are humble, have a contrite spirit and receives the word of God by faith. When received by an individual, the word has the dynamic power to break off every yoke caused by sin and bring, not only physical healing from sickness, but healing from every heartache and deception of the mind/soul. The power of the ministered word of God can provide freedom from emotional slavery and is the provision of eternal salvation.

4) Surely he hath borne our griefs,
and carried our sorrows:
yet we did esteem him stricken,
smitten of God, and afflicted.
5) But he was wounded for our transgressions,
he was bruised for our iniquities: the
chastisement of our peace was upon him;
and with his stripes we are healed.
Isaiah 53: 4-5 (KJV)

WE NEED DELIVERANCE FROM THE FOUR S's:

Sin (Romans 7:21-25)

Sin Defined - transgression of the law, willful, intentional, or deliberate violation of a moral or spiritual principle

Self (Romans 8:3-6, 13, 21)

Self-Defined - one's individual personality, nature or interest, ego, desires, soul

Sickness - Physical and Emotional

(Luke 13:16 & Luke 4:1)

Sickness Defined – illness
Physical - Luke 13:16
Emotional - Luke 4:18

Satan, his demons or influence

(Col. 1:13; Mark 16:17)

Satan & Demons Defined – They are fallen angels or evil spirits that oppose God and his people. Deliverance includes the casting out, off or away an evil spirit or influence

Source: Ministry of Deliverance Manual, Apostle Alton R. Williams, Memphis TN.

I & II Sin and Self – The War Within

1. **We are in a constant battle with our flesh. The Spirit unction's us to do one thing and the mind/body wants us to do just the opposite.**

With my mind, I desire to serve the law of God but my flesh, the law of sin wants to do another:
21) "I find then the principle that evil is present in me, the one who wants to do good. 22) For I joyfully concur with the law of God in the inner man, 23) but I see a different law in the members of my body, waging war against the law of my mind and making me a prisoner of the law of sin which is in my members. 24) Wretched man that I am! Who will set me free from the body of this death? 25) Thanks be to God through Jesus Christ our Lord! So then, on the one hand I myself with my mind am serving the law of God, but on the other, with my flesh the law of sin." Romans 7:21-25 (NASB)

2. **We must walk after the Spirit not the flesh:**

3) "For what the law could not do, in that it was weak through the flesh, God sending his own Son in the likeness of sinful flesh, and for sin, condemned sin in the flesh: 4) That the righteousness of the law might be fulfilled in us, who walk not after the flesh, but after the Spirit. 5) For they that are after the flesh do mind the things of the flesh; but they that are after the Spirit the things of the Spirit. 6) For to be carnally minded is death; but to be spiritually minded is life and peace." Romans 8:3-6 (KJV)

3. **If we live according to the flesh and not by the spirit, it brings death:**

"For if ye live after the flesh, ye shall die: but if ye through the Spirit do mortify the deeds of the body, ye shall live." Romans 8:13 (KJV)

"Because the creature itself also shall be delivered from the bondage of corruption into the glorious liberty of the children of God". Romans 8:21 (KJV)

SELF BRINGS:

Self-pity, accusation, rejection, condemnation and pity, Self-will, rule and selfishness, Self-deception, seduction and delusion, Self-consciousness, analysis, Self-evaluation, and vindication, Self-concern, indulgence, gratification and Self-savior, Self-defeat, reproach, concern, criticism, hatred and flagellation, Self-exaltation, promotion and self-reward

Source: Deliverance from 'Self' By Frank and Ida Mae Hammond

4. **Problems with Sin/Self leads to:**
   - ✓ Guilt
   - ✓ Condemnation
   - ✓ Accusation

- ✓ Torment
- ✓ Strongholds (thinking patterns based on lies and deception that cause us to see God and self incorrectly).

If you were sickly or abused as a child, abused as a spouse; you could spiral into: rebellion, addiction, lust, perversion, mental illness, passivity, doubt or rejection.

5. We must make a decision to give up the things of the flesh.

"In the same way you must give up everything that you have. If you don't, you can't be my disciples." Luke 14:33(NIRV)

"...Love the Lord your God with all your heart and with all your soul and with all your mind. [38] *This is the first and greatest commandment." Matthew. 22:37(NIV)*

"I have been crucified with Christ and I no longer live but Christ lives in me. The life I live in the body, I live by faith in the Son of God, who loved me and gave himself for me." Galatians 2:20 (NIV)

WHAT TO DO REGARDING THE BODY:

- ✓ Present your bodies a living sacrifice.
- ✓ Bind spirits of Lust (lust of the fresh, fornication, adultery).
- ✓ Break Soul Ties – sexual, intimate relations with another individual. We become one with whoever we tie our flesh to. (Matthew 19:5-6, "the two shall be one flesh")

III. We Need Deliverance From: Sickness – Physical and Emotional

Some of us need deliverance from demons that have made us sick. When demons are present, they not only affect the spiritual life of the individual but the body as well.

Illness may have both physical and/or demonic roots.

Many Christians grow closer to God during a personal illness, due to their persistent prayers and faith confessions. This may be an indication that their sickness may not be associated with demons. However, in cases where the sick are not experiencing spiritual growth but getting bitter, angry and more sinful, there is a possibility the sickness has a demonic root. They need more than physical healing. They need deliverance.

Once the offending spirit is cast out of the body, the disease - without its life source - dies.

"And ought not this woman, being a daughter of Abraham, whom Satan hath bound, lo, these eighteen years, be loosed from this bond on the sabbath day?" Luke 13:16 (KJV)

Emotional Healing – "Inner Healing"

A person may need emotional healing, also known as inner healing. "Inner Healing" is healing for a person who has been abused, rejected, wounded or hurt in some way requiring extensive healing in the "seat" of their emotions.

Demons are familiar with our background, situations and experiences. Their responsibility is to plunge hot pokers into every wound we have ever suffered; thus, causing the sores to become inflamed, painful to the touch and to fester. This effect causes physical pain, misery, distress, embarrassment and mutilation. Instead of the wounds being bandaged and made better, the individual never heals. In fact, they become worse. People cannot gain freedom from their past, the present is foggy and their destiny is hindered. This can cause depression, rebellion and other negative outcomes associated with the predicament. The soul of an individual, in this condition, opens and re-opens resulting in demonic spirits entering and re-entering the soul or influencing the mind.

a) Consider an open wound

A physical cut is an injury resulting in a break or opening in the skin. Instead of picturing a cut in the skin, picture this injury to the soul. The injury may be near the surface, deep, smooth or jagged. Also, the wound could be so deep it tears into the tendons, muscles, ligaments, nerves, blood vessels or bone. Wounding emotional cuts/injuries can go deep into the soul. Just like the body, care must be administered emotionally/spiritually for healing to take place.

b) How Can These Wounds Be Healed?

- ✓ Recognize Sin
- ✓ Humble Yourself
- ✓ Confess Your Sin
- ✓ Repent From Sin

- ✓ Forgive Others
- ✓ Deliverance

c) Jesus' suffering holds provision for our healing

"We can reach out to Jesus and receive the promises of healing and deliverance from suffering and sickness. In the same way, we can turn to Jesus for salvation. We can expect him to hear our requests in the area of sickness."

"That it might be fulfilled which was spoken by Esaias the prophet, saying, Himself took our infirmities, and bare our sicknesses." Matthew 8:17 (KJV)

"Who his own self bare our sins in his own body on the tree that we, being dead to sins, should live unto righteousness: by whose stripes ye were healed." I Peter 2:24 (KJV)

"Paul reminded early believers that their forgetfulness of the provisions of the Cross were causing some to experience a premature death" (I Cor. 11:24-30).

23-26 *Let me go over with you again exactly what goes on in the Lord's Supper and why it is so centrally important. I received my instructions from the Master himself and passed them on to you. The Master, Jesus, on the night of his betrayal, took bread. Having given thanks, he broke it and said,*

This is my body, broken for you.
Do this to remember me.

After supper, he did the same thing with the cup:

This cup is my blood, my new covenant with you.
Each time you drink this cup, remember me.

What you must solemnly realize is that every time you eat this bread and every time you drink this cup, you reenact in your words and actions the death of the Master. You will be drawn back to this meal again and again until the Master returns. You must never let familiarity breed contempt.

27-28 *Anyone who eats the bread or drinks the cup of the Master irreverently is like part of the crowd that jeered and spit on him at his death. Is that the kind of "remembrance" you want to be part of? Examine your motives, test your heart, come to this meal in holy awe.*

29-32 *If you give no thought (or worse, don't care) about the broken body of the Master when you eat and drink, you're running the risk of serious consequences. That's why so many of you even now are listless and sick, and others have gone to an early grave. If we get this straight now, we won't have to be straightened out later on. Better to be confronted by the Master now than to face a fiery confrontation later.*

"Forget not all His benefits: who forgives all your iniquities, who heals all your diseases" (Ps. 103:2, 3).
Source: Jack Hayford - Deliverance from Suffering and Sickness

IV. We Need Deliverance From Satan, His Influence and Demons

One of the major areas Christians need deliverance in relates to sexual sin.

Note: there are Sexual Demons:

- ✓ Incubus – an evil spirit lies on a person in their sleep. Spirit takes on the form of a man.
- ✓ Succubus – demon takes on a female form to have intercourse with male.
- ✓ Seducing Spirits, Whoredom, Perverse Spirits, etc.

1. Remove Legal Rights

There are things that give demons legal permission to enter and remain in our lives. Before demons can be cast out, it is important to address and remove these legal rights. Failure to remove legal rights can hinder deliverance. (Some examples: Voodoo dolls, video games, books dealing with pornography or the occult)

2. Remove Strongholds

Tearing down strongholds is a major part of a deliverance ministry. Strongholds are incorrect thinking patterns people develop over time. They are often set up and nurtured by demons through lies and deception. Demons thrive on strongholds and use them to hang around a person and torment them. (Some examples: atheism, unbelief, stealing, greed, alcohol addiction, drugs, sexual sin, promiscuity, pornography and homosexuality)

DELIVERANCE AND AUTHORITY

YOU HAVE POWER AND AUTHORITY AS A BELIEVER!

What is Power?

- ✓ Power means strength and ability

What is Delegated Authority?

- ✓ Delegated authority is the power entrusted to another

What is Authority?

- ✓ Authority is the right to use the Power (i.e., the Mayor of the city delegates power to both policemen and firemen)

Do not allow the enemy to bring you under condemnation, guilt, torment or deception regarding sin. Keep away from the things that contribute/cause sin. This usually requires a Christian to activate their authority. First they must know they have authority and then act in faith on that authority.

The power of our authority rests on the power that is behind that authority. God has delegated that authority to us. We have been commissioned, by God, to use that authority. Because of the blood of Jesus, we have the power of God behind that authority; therefore, we can exercise this authority and win.

[7] Submit yourselves therefore to God. Resist the devil, and he will flee from you. James 4:7 (KJV)

[7] And as ye go, preach, saying, The kingdom of heaven is at hand. [8] Heal the sick, cleanse the lepers, raise the dead, cast out devils: freely ye have received, freely give. Matthew 10:7-8 (KJV)

- ✓ We are commanded to use this authority – John 14:2
- ✓ Jesus was sent to earth where He was authority - Luke 4:18
- ✓ Jesus came to earth to delegate this authority - Matthew 10:1
- ✓ Jesus gave the church instruction regarding the use of this authority - Mark 16:17

GOD DECLARES IN ISAIAH 61:1-3 – HE WANTS US FREE!

The Spirit of the Lord God is upon me, because the Lord has anointed and qualified me to preach the Gospel of Good tidings to the meek, the poor, and afflicted; He has sent me to bind up and heal the brokenhearted, to proclaim liberty to the (physical and spiritual) captives and to open the prison and eyes of those who are bound.- To proclaim the acceptable year of the Lord (the year of favor) and the day of vengeance of our God. To comfort all who mourn. To grant (consolidation and joy) to those who mourn in Zion - to give them an ornament (a garland of diadem) of beauty instead of mourning, the garment (expressive) of praise instead of a heavy, burdened and failing spirit, that they may be called oaks of righteousness (lofty, strong, and magnificent, distinguished for uprightness, justice, and right standing with God), the planting of the Lord, that He may be glorified.

...For this purpose was the Son of God manifested, that he might destroy the works of the devil... I John 3:8 (KJV)

MAIN HIERARCHY OF SPIRITS – THE (16) STRONGMEN OF THE BIBLE

There are (16) demonic strongmen identified in the Bible.

These spirits dominate and control other lesser spirits and demonic powers that come under their domain. We must identify and bind these strongmen and their cohorts. We bind the negative aspects associated with these spirits and loose the positive according to Matthew 18:18.

[18]"Assuredly, I say to you, whatever you bind on earth will be bound in heaven, and whatever you loose on earth will be loosed in heaven." (NKJV)

We want to ensure when we evict the enemy from our lives we replace him with the spirit of God. We do not want the spirits to come back to an empty space, bringing more demons then before with them.

And Jesus knew their thoughts, and said unto them: 29) *Or else how can one enter into a strong man's house, and spoil his goods, except he first bind the strong man? and then he will spoil his house. Matthew 12:29 (KJV)*

(16) Demonic Strongmen Identified

1. **Spirit of Antichrist**

   John 4:2-3

   All spirits that attack or undermine the divinity of Christ, blasphemes against the Holy Spirit, prosecute and attack Christians.

2. **Spirit of Bondage**

   Romans 8:15, 2 Peter 2:19, 2 Tim. 2:26

   All spirits that control and enslave you to the point that you become useless to the kingdom of God and slaves to the kingdom of darkness.

3. **Deaf and Dumb Spirit**

   Mark 9:17-26

   All spirits related to both physical/mental and spiritual ability to physically and spiritually hear and speak. This Spirit is also associated with the unclean, vexing spirit of insanity.

4. **Familiar Spirits**

   Deut. 18:10-12, Leviticus 19:31, Leviticus 20: 6, Leviticus 20:27

   The practice of calling on the dead, by an individual, sorcerers, mediums or necromancers with the purpose of answering questions, foretelling the future or other related occult activities.

5. **Spirit of Fear**

   2 Timothy 1:7, Isaiah 41:13

   All spirits related to phobias, fears and anxieties that leave a person in physical and mental bondage and torment.

6. **Spirit of Heaviness**

   Isaiah 61:3

   All spirits related to despair, gloom, grief, depression, oppression and suicide.

7. **Spirit of Infirmity**

   Luke 13:11

   All spirits that may be related to any form of chronic sickness and disease.

8. Spirit of Jealousy

Proverbs 6:34, Numbers 5:14

All spirits of extreme competition, anger, revenge, rage, hatred, murder and profanity resulting in a person feeling threatened, insecure, or challenged by another's success which may or may not be real but imagined.

9. Lying Spirit

2 Chron. 18:22, Proverbs 12:22

All spirits that make lies appear like the truth, where the main intent is to deceive the individual, i.e., religious spirit, vanity, homosexuality, adultery, double standards (hypocrisy), superstition and self-deception.

10. Perverse Spirit

Isaiah 19:14

All spirits that relate to lust, fornication, adultery, sexual perversion (sexual troubles), homosexuality, pornography, a wounded spirit and corruption.

11. Spirit of Pride

Proverbs 16:18

All spirits of arrogance, gossip, stubbornness, self-righteousness, mocking of others and control (witchcraft).

12. Spirit of Divination

Acts16:16

The practice of endeavoring to foretell the future or future events, trying to discover unseen knowledge by supernatural or occultist means.

13. Spirit of Whoredom

Hosea 5:4

Unfaithfulness/adultery, spirit/soul/ or body prostitution, love of money, excessive appetite, fornication, chronic dissatisfaction, idolatry and worldliness.

14. Seducing Spirits

1John 4:1&3

Spirits related to a hypocritical, seductive, lying, seared conscience, deceptive, fascination to evil ways, objects or person, attractions - fascination by false prophets, signs and wonders, etc., wanderers from the truth, seducers and enticers.

15. Spirit of Error

I John 4:6, Psalms 51:10

All spirits related to worldly motivation. Spirits that are un-submissive, un-teachable, defensive/argumentative. This spirit defends false doctrines, servant of corruption, contentions and new age teaching.

16. Spirit of Death

I Cor. 15:26

All spirits related to chronic sickness unto death, despair and suicide unto death, tormenting and murdering spirits unto death. Source: Based on Ezine Article, *"What Are The 16 Strongman Spirits" by Kimberly M. Snyder*

WITCHCRAFT & SORCERY

Individuals involved in witchcraft and sorcery should go through deliverance. Witchcraft and sorcery is used to provide knowledge through supernatural means about events, people and situations. We have presented several types, in different categories, for you to review:

Witchcraft

Palm Reading, Fortunetelling, Psychics, Ouija Boards, Horoscope, Martial Arts

Sorcery

Drugs, Potions, Charms, Amulets, Magic, Spells, Incantations, various forms of music

False Religion

Mormons, Christian Science, Hare-Krishna, Buddhism, Islam, Unitarianism, Freemasonry, Unification Church, Moonies, Baha'ism, Rosicrucian' Theosophy, Unity, Urantia, Subud

Most false religions denounce the following basic biblical beliefs:

- ✓ Jesus came to save us from our sins – *Luke 9:56*
- ✓ Jesus was born of a Virgin - *Matthew 1:23-25*
- ✓ Jesus was Sinless - *Hebrews 4:15*
- ✓ Jesus is God – *Matthew 1:23, John 1:1*

- ✓ Jesus is the Son of God - *John 3:38*
- ✓ Jesus died and rose from the dead - *Romans 10:9*
- ✓ Jesus ascended into heaven, seated on the right hand of God, making intercession for us and is coming back again - *Acts 2:34, Hebrew 1:13, Hebrews 7:25, Thess. 5:1-4)*

  Source: Ministry of Deliverance Manual, Apostle Alton R. Williams, Memphis TN.

29) In those days they shall say no more, The fathers have eaten a sour grape, and the children's teeth are set on edge. 30) But every one shall die for his own iniquity: every man that eateth the sour grape, his teeth shall be set on edge. Jeremiah 31:29-30 (KJV

Thou shewest loving kindness unto thousands, and recompensest the iniquity of the fathers into the bosom of their children after them: the Great, the Mighty God, the LORD of hosts, is his name. Jeremiah 32:18 (KJV)

CASTING OUT OF DEVILS

Defined as commanding unclean spirits or evil spirits to leave an individual or individuals. Command spirits to go into dry and desolate places, never to return. *(Review remaining chapters for a complete overview in this area).* Casting out demons requires faith, humility, authority and sometimes fasting.

COMMONLY ASKED QUESTIONS ABOUT DELIVERANCE

Can Christians Be Possessed?
No. A Christian cannot be owned by demons.
Note: Possessed equals ownership.

Can a Christian have Demons?
Yes, just like they can have a sickness or disease. Christians are composed of three parts: Spirit, Body and Soul. The Spirit of a man belongs to God. A man's spirit is joined with the Holy Spirit. The Body and Soul can still be influenced by Satan and his demons. Once saved, Christians must renew their mind with the word of God. As the mind begins to line up with the spirit of God, the body and soul will also.

How can Demons Gain Access to a Believer?
Either the demons were there before the person came to Christ - through lifestyle, generational curses, and bondages or through vows they made with the enemy.

Or

The demons entered after a person became born again through open doors, (i.e.) unforgiveness, bitterness, offense, sexual sin, soul ties and where bondages are passed from one person to another.

"Neither give place to the devil". Ephesians 4:27 (KJV)

*"Lest Satan should get an advantage of us:
for we are not ignorant of his devices". 2 Cor. 2:11
(KJV)*

Should demons be cast out of unbelievers?
Casting a demon out of an unbeliever is not wise. Always ask a person if they have accepted Jesus Christ as Lord and Savior. An unbeliever has given Satan the legal right to inhibit their space. Demons legal rights can only be cut off if and when a person gets saved. Demons can become very violent and dangerous to unbelievers and nearby people. Unbelievers have no covering, no blood protection and no hedge. Once a demon is cast out of an unbeliever, the demons will return and the "latter end, of the unbeliever, will be worse than their beginning". First, lead the person to Jesus and then cast the devil(s) out. For the Bible reminds us that,

43) "*When the unclean spirit is gone out of a man, he walketh through dry places, seeking rest, and findeth none. 44) Then he saith, I will return into my house from whence I came out; and when he is come, he findeth it empty, swept, and garnished. 45) Then goeth he, and*

taketh with himself seven other spirits more wicked than himself, and they enter in and dwell there: and the last state of that man is worse than the first. Even so shall it be also unto this wicked generation." Matthew 12:43-45 (KJV)

When is Fasting and Prayer Necessary for Deliverance?

If one is having a planned deliverance service or session, one might want to fast. Since deliverance is not always planned, one should always lead a fasted, prayerful life.

17) "And one of the multitude answered and said, Master, I have brought unto thee my son, which hath a dumb spirit; 18) And wheresoever he taketh him, he teareth him: and he foameth, and gnasheth with his teeth, and pineth away: and I spake to thy disciples that they should cast him out; and they could not. 19) He answereth him, and saith, O faithless generation, how long shall I be with you? how long shall I suffer you? bring him unto me. 20) And they brought him unto him: and when he saw him, straightway the spirit tare him; and he fell on the ground, and wallowed foaming. 21) And he asked his father, How long is it ago since this came unto him? And he said, of a child. 22) And oftentimes it hath cast him into the fire, and into the waters, to destroy him: but if thou canst do anything, have compassion on us, and help us. 23) Jesus said unto him, If thou canst believe, all things are possible to him that believeth 24) And straightway the father of the child cried out, and said with tears, Lord, I believe; help thou mine unbelief. 25) When Jesus saw that the people came running together, he rebuked the foul spirit, saying unto him, Thou dumb and deaf spirit, I charge thee, come out of him, and enter no more into him. 26) And the spirit cried, and rent him sore, and came *out of him: and he was as one dead; insomuch that many said, He is dead. 27) But Jesus took him by the hand, and lifted him up; and he arose. 28) And when he was come into the house, his disciples asked him privately, Why could not we cast him out? 29) And he said unto them, This kind can come forth by nothing, but by prayer and fasting". Mark 9:17-29(KJV)*

Can Demons enter a child?

Yes, it is possible for demons to enter a child and stay dormant for years without a physical manifestation.

CHAPTER 6

Starting Deliverance at Home - Spiritual House

Graven images of their gods shall ye burn with fire: thou shalt not desire the silver or gold that is on them, nor take it unto thee, lest thou be snared therein: for it is an abomination to the LORD thy God. Neither shalt thou bring an abomination into thine house, lest thou be a cursed thing like it: but thou shalt utterly detest it, and thou shalt utterly abhor it; for it is a cursed thing.
Deuteronomy 7:25-26

STARTING DELIVERANCE AT HOME – Spiritual House Cleaning

We encounter spirits/demons in (3) ways:

1. **Visitation** - Spirits will show up in or around people we know or interact with. They simply come in uninvited. They will go and stay with a person or family for a period of time. Demons do not need an invitation to come in. They must be cast out in order to get rid of them.

2. **Habitation** - Spirits will inhabit a place where demons have been assigned, like a house, government building, mortuary, school, etc. Habitation can occur as a result of willful sin by the people occupying the place. Demons can even occupy the land on which the building is located. Spirits can also be attracted by things such as statues, art, jewelry, certain types of music and books. It is, for this reason, important to remove things that attract or enable them to stay. Certain inanimate objects may attract or provide an open door for demonic habitation.

3. **Infiltration** - More than anything, spirits want to occupy an actual person. Given an open door/gate, a person can be influenced and even controlled by demon spirits. Demons do not ask a person if they can influence or control them. They look for an open door such as sin, weakness, etc. in which they can seduce a person. When the circumstances are right, an individual will freely participate in an activity that will subsequently allow the enemy to enter one's gate. "An individual has five gates, in his flesh, in which the devil can enter"/influence. They are sight, smell, sound, touch and taste. Identify the type of territorial, familiar and seducing spirits by the type of activities exhibited. Source: based on Chris Ward, D. Min, Why are we so Ignorant of Demons, 1999.

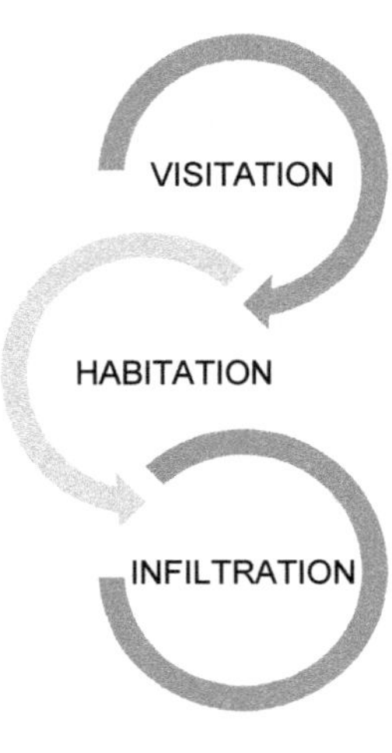

FIRST THINGS FIRST – Getting Rid of Accursed Things

We want to rid our homes of the (cursed) objects or things that attract demon spirits which causes us to be cursed by God. If you have a cursed object in your possession, you become cursed by God! Destroy items by breaking, burning or at least throwing them in the trash. Do not keep the cursed silver or gold. If the cursed object belongs to someone else and it is in your home, let them know how you feel. Simply state, you no longer want the item in your home. Anoint the object with oil and get rid of it. Anoint your house with oil and drive out evil spirits from your house and possessions.

And ye, in any wise keep yourselves from the accursed thing, lest ye make yourselves accursed, when ye take of the accursed thing, and make the camp of Israel a curse, and trouble it. Joshua 6:18 (KJV)

Immediately Remove From Your Home the Following:

- ✓ Good luck charms and amulets, fetish objects - any object, idea, eliciting unquestioning reverence, respect, or devotion, jewelry used in occult worship or dedications,

- ✓ Penthouse, Hustler and Playboy magazines, pornography
- ✓ Halloween costumes
- ✓ Ouija Boards
- ✓ Dungeons and Dragons, Masters of the Universe games, other videos with eastern religious music, and un-interpreted languages. etc.
- ✓ Artifacts from Buddhist, Hindu and other eastern religions, items used in meditation Some (usually authentic) Southwest Indian art and African art
- ✓ Books on Satanism, witchcraft, the New Age Movement
- ✓ Books and items related to horoscopes and astrology
- ✓ Certain comic books, rock posters, hard rock posters, and other materials with images of darkness, violence or sorcery
- ✓ Art with obvious demonic representations such as snakes and dragons
- ✓ Materials related to Mormonism, Jehovah Witnesses, the Unity Church, and other cults as well as secret societies like Freemasonry, Eastern Star and similar societies
- ✓ Video games with demonic and witchcraft reference material and images
- ✓ Movies with occult or supernatural messages
- ✓ Idols, gods of any kind
- ✓ Movies with extreme violence or gore

Removal of Inanimate Objects

Ask God to reveal to you the things He deems "accursed things" and remove them immediately from your home and or personal work space. For non-personal spaces, do not remove the property of others, discreetly anoint object and space with oil, and break the powers over the object. Cancel the assignment of the accursed thing over your life and the lives of others.

- ✓ Destroy all objects dedicated to demons (such as idols and artifacts).
- ✓ Verbally denounce Satan, his power and demon cohorts.
- ✓ Claim authority as a believer using the name of Jesus Christ and the authority of His shed blood.
- ✓ Anoint the door post and window sills with oil.
- ✓ Open the window and doors as you command the spirits to go and shut them firmly.

Step by Step Process For Land and House Cleansing

- **Be led by the Holy Spirit. Identify the problems that are occurring in your home.**
- **Set aside an adequate amount of time to pray over**

the location.

- **Find scriptures that specifically address the issues in your home or life.**
- **Remove all distractions, TV, etc.**
- **Search your home and possessions for cursed objects.** Remove the accursed thing from your house. If you cannot destroy someone else's possessions, anoint the object with oil break the power the object appears to hold.
- **Before you clean house, forgive others, break all soul ties, known curses and psychic prayers made against you, your family, etc.**
- **Praise God**, **cover** yourself and your family **with the blood of Jesus** and **pray** a prayer of **protection** over you, your spouse, your children, pets, relatives and friends who live on your land and/or house.
- **Use anointing oil** (blessed olive oil) and anoint your land, doors, windows and walls in individual rooms and drive spirits out. Work your way from the back to the front of the land/house.

- **Open windows and doors and sweep them out.** After anointing your house, take a physical broom and symbolically sweep your house clean, opening your door and kicking the devil out.
- **Command spirits to go to dry and desolate places to return no more.**
- **Decree authority scriptures and speak them out loud.** There is more power to speaking out loud than reading or praying silently. Pray some of the scriptures, included in this handbook, as you exercise your authority to spiritually clean house. Profess the scriptures in your prayer. Pray and anoint as you walk through your house to rid your home of Satan and his cohorts.
- Anoint as you walk on the land or through your house to rid your home of Satan and his cohorts.
- **Dispatch angels in your home.**
- **End by praising God and thanking him for the victory.**

Pray as often as needed until house, building or land is cleansed.

Use the following scriptures to support and war over your house. Read them out loud as you go through your house. Personalize the scriptures.

Example: *"I have been given authority over all the power of the enemy. Therefore, I cast out Satan and his cohorts who have entered this home, in Jesus' name".*

House Cleansing Scriptures

"As for you, watch yourselves in the city under holy curse. Be careful that you don't covet anything in it and take something that's cursed, endangering the camp of Israel with the curse and making trouble for everyone. All silver and gold, all vessels of bronze and iron are holy to GOD. Put them in GOD's treasury." Joshua 6:18-19 (MSG)

19) "Many of them also which used curious arts brought their books together, and burned them before all men: and they counted the price of them, and found it fifty thousand pieces of silver. 20) So mightily grew the word of God and prevailed". Acts 19: 19-20 (KJV)

25-26) "Make sure you set fire to their carved gods. Don't get greedy for the veneer of silver and gold on them and take it for yourselves—you'll get trapped by it for sure. GOD hates it; it's an abomination to GOD, your God. And don't dare bring one of these abominations home or you'll end up just like it, burned up as a holy destruction. No: It is forbidden! Hate it. Abominate it. Destroy it and preserve GOD's holiness". Deuteronomy 7:25-26 (MSG)

Authority Scriptures

*"Behold, **I have given you authority over all the power of the enemy** and to tread upon serpents and scorpions, and nothing shall injure you". Luke 10:19*

"For our struggle is not against flesh and blood, but against the rulers, against the powers, against the world forces of this darkness, against the spiritual forces of wickedness in the heavenly places". Ephesians 6:12

*"**And they overcame him because of the blood of the Lamb** and because of the word of their testimony, and they did not love their life even to death". Revelation 12:11*

"The angel of the Lord encamps around those who fear Him, and rescues them". Psalm 37:7

"And whatever you ask in My name, that will I do, that the Father may be glorified in the Son. If you ask Me anything in My name, I will do it". John 14:13-14

Important Prayer Review Points - for House Cleaning

- ✓ Praise God for his sovereignty
- ✓ Ask God to cleanse your land/home of every unclean spirit and command them to be gone forever. Send every spirit to dry desolate places, never to return again.
- ✓ Bind every demon that has invaded your house and loose angels in your home.
- ✓ Apply the blood of Jesus to every room, dispatch warring angels and pray protection over self, spouse, children, other relatives, friends and pets. Use the word of God to evict every spirit not of God.
- ✓ Put on the full amour of God
- ✓ Praise God for a clean house

CHAPTER 7

Curses: Defined, Revealed and Broken

Curses cannot hurt you unless you deserve them. They are like birds that fly by and never light. *Proverbs 26:2 (GNT)*

CURSES - Defined, Revealed and Broken

Curses are God's recompense in the life of a person for sin. While God does not curse believers, the sins of the believer can be the cause for the curse. The Bible states, we reap what we sow and that the wages of sin is death. Therefore, it is important for a believer to live holy lives and not willingly participate in a life of sin. The Bible also states, that a curse causeless shall not come. In other words, no cause, no curse. Curses can cause damage, destruction and ruin for several generations, which can cause a "sorrow of the heart".

[64] Render unto them a recompence O Lord, according to the work of their hands. [65] Give them sorrow of heart, thy curse unto them. [66] Persecute and destroy them in anger from under the heavens of the Lord. Lamentations 3:64-66 (KJV)

Believers are no longer under the curse of the law or curses. Jesus has redeemed us from all curses. But let me preference that statement by saying, we are not under a curse unless we or our descendants have willfully disobeyed and open the doors for evil spirits to enter and perpetuate their workings in our lives and the lives of our families. There are some sins that may cause a curse, i.e., the sin of idolatry and iniquity/perversion can be the cause for a curse, but not every sin is the cause for a curse. Examples of perversions that could cause curses include: financial, religious, spiritual, behavioral, the spoken word, and sexual.

There is a difference between the curse of the law and curses. The Jewish people had over 600 mosaic laws which they were expected to obey. No one could keep all those laws and if they were to break one law, they were condemned. These were the perquisite requirement of God before Jesus became the fulfillment of that law. Christ was obedient in life, in his death on the cross and in the resurrection. We now have continued access to the Father by faith. The law was the shadow of things to come. Since individuals could not fulfill the law, God gave us a better substitute, Jesus Christ, who took away the sins of the world. Note that although he took away the sins of everybody, we still must individually believe, confess and accept, by faith, the redemptive works done for us on that cross. We also have to appropriate that same faith for healing, deliverance and the release from curses.

9-10 So those now who live by faith are blessed along with Abraham, who lived by faith—this is no new doctrine! And that means that anyone who tries to live by his own effort, independent of God, is doomed to failure. Scripture backs this up: "Utterly cursed is every person who fails to carry out every detail written in the Book of the law."[11-12] *The obvious impossibility of carrying out such a moral program should make it plain that no one can sustain a relationship with God that way. The person who lives in right relationship with God does it by embracing what God arranges for him. Doing things for God is the opposite of entering into what God does for you. Habakkuk had it right: "The person who believes God, is set right by God—and that's the real life." Rule-keeping does not naturally evolve into living by faith, but only perpetuates itself in more and more rule-keeping, a fact observed in Scripture: "The one who does these things [rule-keeping] continues to live by them."* [13-14] *Christ redeemed us from that self-defeating, cursed life by absorbing it completely into himself. Do you remember the Scripture that says, "Cursed is everyone who hangs on a tree"? That is what happened when Jesus was nailed to the cross: He became a curse, and at the same time dissolved the curse. And now, because of that, the air is cleared and we can see that Abraham's blessing is present and available for non-Jews, too. We are all able to receive God's life, his Spirit, in and with us by believing—just the way Abraham received it. Galatians 3:9-14 (MSG)*

Not every principle taught in the Old Testament was done away with. One such principle is that of sin and consequences in the life of the believer. There is no way to positively identify whether an individual is or is not operating under a curse unless it is revealed by the Holy Spirit. However, the continued harassment of the saints by Satan in a specific area such as chronic, reoccurring problems can be a clue. Curses affect the lives of believers as well as unbelievers. If you don't believe in curses and there is no habitual sin in your life, still make it a point to cover yourself with the blood of Jesus, exhibit wisdom in the conduct of your daily lives and care with the people in which you daily interact. If all else fails, ask God to reveal whether there is a curse on you and your family line, repent and break the curse.

Thou shewest loving kindness unto thousands, and recompensest the iniquity of the fathers into the bosom of their children after them: the Great, the Mighty God, the LORD of hosts, is his name. Jeremiah 32:18 (KJV)

Types of Curses:

1) **Generational Curses** – The Bible indicates that curses may not start with a current generation but the curse may be payment for the sins of a former generation. A curse in a family line does not die with the person it may have started with. That curse can visit a family up to and beyond the fourth generation. Generational curses are judgments passed on to an individual because of the sins perpetuated in a family, ethnic group,

etc., for several generations. These curses, often associated with familiar spirits, can go from one generation to another because of the disobedience of mothers and fathers, grandparents, great grandparents and earlier generations. Individuals are often influenced to commit those same sins of their past generations. The consequences of those sins will affect future generations.

[5] Thou shalt not bow down thyself to them, nor serve them: for I the LORD thy God am a jealous God, visiting the iniquity of the fathers upon the children unto the third and fourth generation of them that hate me; Exodus 20:5 (KJV)

[7] Keeping mercy for thousands, forgiving iniquity and transgression and sin, and that will by no means clear the guilty; visiting the iniquity of the fathers upon the children, and upon the children's children, unto the third and to the fourth generation. Exodus 34:7 (KJV)

[3] Thou shalt have no other gods before me. [4] Thou shalt not make unto thee any graven image, or any likeness of any thing that is in heaven above, or that is in the earth beneath, or that is in the water under the earth. [5] Thou shalt not bow down thyself to them, nor serve them: for I the LORD thy God am a jealous God, visiting the iniquity

of the fathers upon the children unto the third and fourth generation of them that hate me; Exodus 21:3-5 (KJV)

[1] *And as Jesus passed by, he saw a man which was blind from his birth.* [2] *And his disciples asked him, saying, Master, who did sin, this man, or his parents, that he was born blind?* [3] *Jesus answered, Neither hath this man sinned, nor his parents: but that the works of God should be made manifest in him. John 9:1-3 (KJV)*

It is not God's desire to punish children, but it is simply evidence that "sin can be passed down from one generation to the next". For example, if a child has a father who is an alcoholic and they become an alcoholic and their children and children's children become alcoholics', we thus, witness the effects of a never ending cycle of sin. This may be an indication of a generational curse. The same principle is also ascribed for poverty, having children out of wedlock (Deut. 23:2), etc.

CHILDREN CAN CHOOSE TO OBEY GOD AND LIVE DIFFERENTLY FROM THEIR PARENTS.

[19] *Yet say ye, Why? doth not the son bear the iniquity of the father? When the son hath done that which is lawful and right, and hath kept all my statutes, and hath done*

them, he shall surely live. [20] *The soul that sinneth, it shall die. The son shall not bear the iniquity of the father, neither shall the father bear the iniquity of the son: the righteousness of the righteous shall be upon him, and the wickedness of the wicked shall be upon him.* [21] *But if the wicked will turn from all his sins that he hath committed, and keep all my statutes, and do that which is lawful and right, he shall surely live, he shall not die.* [22] *All his transgressions that he hath committed, they shall not be mentioned unto him: in his righteousness that he hath done he shall live. Ezekiel 18:19-22 (KJV)*

[4] *But he slew not their children, but did as it is written in the law in the book of Moses, where the Lord commanded, saying, The fathers shall not die for the children, neither shall the children die for the fathers, but every man shall die for his own sin.*
2 Chronicles 25:4 (KJV)

- ✓ The price for *generational curses* was paid by Christ on the cross.

- ✓ The one cure for generational curses is repentance.

2) **Spoken Curses** - Words can bring curses or blessings. Negative words, when spoken about ourselves, can bring curses. Examples include statements like:

- I will never amount to anything.
- I don't believe I'm not going to live a long life.
- If not for bad luck, I wouldn't have any luck at all.
- I am ugly.
- No one loves me.
- God cannot use someone like me.

"But I say unto you, That every idle word that men shall speak, they shall give account thereof in the day of judgment." Matthew 12:36 (KJV)

"But shun profane and vain babblings: for they will increase unto more ungodliness." 2 Timothy 2:16 (KJV)

- Speaking against the prophet, pastor and anointed one of God brings a curse.

  "Saying, Touch not mine anointed, and do my prophets no harm." Psalm 105:15 (KJV)

3) **Curses from Serving Idol Gods and Self** – God has always stated that He was a jealous God and not only would He not share His glory with us, but He will not share His glory with other Gods. One would think that the God of the universe has the right to set things up anyway he sees fit. As humans, we just need to adjust to the fact that God is a sovereign God.

3 Thou shalt have no other gods before me. 4 Thou shalt not make unto thee any graven image, or any likeness of anything that is in heaven above, or that is in the earth beneath, or that is in the water under the earth.
5 Thou shalt not bow down thyself to them, nor serve them: for I the LORD thy God am a jealous God, visiting the iniquity of the fathers upon the children unto the third and fourth generation of them that hate me;
Exodus 20:3-5 (KJV)

[16] Lest ye corrupt yourselves, and make you a graven image, the similitude of any figure, the likeness of male or female, [17] The likeness of any beast that is on the earth, the likeness of any winged fowl that flieth in the air, [18] The likeness of any thing that creepeth on the ground, the likeness of any fish that is in the waters beneath the earth:
Deut. 4:15-16 (KJV)

[5] Thus saith the LORD; Cursed be the man that trusteth in man, and maketh flesh
his arm, and whose heart departeth from the LORD. Jeremiah 17:5 (KJV)

4) **Cursing Israel** – The Jewish nation is the lineage that God chose to bring his son to the earth. We can choose to be in favor of God's elect or not. God wants us to pray for Israel as well as bless them.

[3] And I will bless them that bless thee, and curse him that curseth thee: and in thee shall all families of the earth be blessed. Genesis 12:3 (KJV)

[6] Pray for the peace of Jerusalem: they shall prosper that love thee. Psalm 122:6 (KJV)

5) **Ties with the Occult** – The use of witchcraft and sorcery can bring a curse upon an individual or family line. It is also used to provide knowledge, through supernatural means, about events, people and situations and placing of curses on others. Some examples are:

✓ **Witchcraft** - Palm reading, fortunetelling, psychics, Ouija Boards, horoscope, martial arts, potions, charms, amulets, magic, spells, incantations, various forms of music

✓ **False Religion** – Mormons, Christian Science, Hare-Krishna, Buddhism, Islam, Unitarianism, Freemasonry, Unification Church, Moonies, Baha'ism, Rosicrucian' Theosophy, Unity, Urantia, Subud, and others

10 There shall not be found among you any one that maketh his son or his daughter to pass through the fire, or that useth divination, or an observer of times, or an enchanter, or a witch. 11 Or a charmer, or a consulter with familiar spirits, or a wizard, or a necromancer 12 For all that do these things are an abomination unto the LORD: and because of these abominations the LORD thy God doth drive them out from before thee. 13 Thou shalt be perfect with the LORD thy God. Deuteronomy 18:10-13 (KJV)

6) **Other Causes for Curses:** Disrespect for parents, illicit sex, non-payment of the tithe, stealing, perverting the gospel, injustice to the weak, treachery against a neighbor, speaking against God's anointed.

7) **The Blessing and Curses of Deuteronomy 28:**

- ✓ Exaltation/Humiliation
- ✓ Children/Barrenness
- ✓ Health/Sickness
- ✓ Prosperity/Poverty
- ✓ Victory/Defeat
- ✓ Head and not the tail/ Tail and not the head
- ✓ Above and not beneath/Beneath and not above

Indications of curses include: chronic financial problems, mental problems, chronic sickness and female problems, chronic accidents, chronic martial/relationship problems and abuse, vagabond condition and premature death.

Solution to Breaking a Curse:

1. Recognize the root cause of the sin
2. Confess known sins to God
3. Repent for your sins and the sins of your ancestors (parents, grandparents, etc.)

4. Break curses placed on you for your personal sin, or for the sin of your ancestors
5. Cover yourself in the blood of Jesus
6. Obey the commands of God

OTHER – SOUL TIES

Soul ties is the knitting or binding together of two (2) or more people through sex, close relationships, blood ties, promises, vows and covenants. Soul ties become spiritual bondages that must be broken in the spirit before an individual can become physically free. Soul ties give the enemy legal right to invade and influence the thoughts and behavior of an individual. Soul ties can be good or bad, as shown in the examples below:

Husband and Wife (Marriage Covenant)

*[5] and said, 'For this reason a man shall leave his father and mother and be joined to his wife, and the two shall become one flesh'? Matthew 19:**5** (NRSV)*

Jonathan's Soul Tie with David (Close Friendship)

18 When David had finished speaking to Saul, the soul of Jonathan was bound to the soul of David, and Jonathan loved him as his own soul. 1 Samuel 18:1 (NRSV)

Relationships based on sexual, mental or physical abuse are considered ungodly ties that need to be broken.

[17] "Then the Babylonians came to her, into the bed of love, And they defiled her with their immorality; So she was defiled by them, and alienated herself from them. *Ezekiel 23:17 (NKJV)*

[2] And when Shechem the son of Hamor the Hivite, prince of the country, saw her, he took her and lay with her, and violated her. [3] His soul was strongly attracted to Dinah the daughter of Jacob, and he loved the young woman and spoke kindly to the young woman. *Genesis 34:2-3 (NKJV)*

Soul ties give the enemy a legal right to influence, hurt and cause harm to an individual.

How to Break a Soul Tie

1. Repent of sins
2. Forgive anyone involved in the relationship
3. Get rid of any ungodly practices, gifts that continue to bind you to that relationship.
4. Verbally renounce any vows made with those individuals.
5. Use your authority and the name of Jesus to renounce any soul ties.

"In Jesus' name, I now renounce any ungodly soul ties formed between myself and ______ as a result of ________________ (sin, covenants, fornication, etc.) in Jesus' name."

Prayer for Breaking Curses:

In the name and power of the blood of Jesus, I renounce and break all curses caused by my sin. I break and sever every sin handed down to me by my ancestors (list the sin(s) and the person's name if known). I now loose myself and my future generations from any bondage passed down to me from my ancestors. I decree and declare that I am free from all curses and all my children and children's children are free from all curses, in Jesus' name. Amen

- ❖ Repeat steps as many times as needed until you have experienced complete freedom from demonic attacks.

CHAPTER 8

for

Ministering

Deliverance

As each one has received a gift, minister it to one another, as good stewards of the manifold grace of God. *1 Peter 4:8-10 (NKJV)*

Guidelines for Ministering Deliverance

Do not try to force deliverance on individuals who do not want to be helped.

- Deliverance performed in a church should be under the covering of the pastor, bishop, apostle, evangelist or teacher. All saints need a spiritual covering.

- Anyone ministering deliverance should be absolutely sure that their lives line up with the word of God. Individuals ministering deliverance and living in sin could halt the success of the entire deliverance process and open themselves up to the transference of spirits. Thus, the deliverance minister should ensure they are not practicing sin, have un-confessed sin and that the guilt of sin has been removed. The God of the Bible is not a God of condemnation but according to scripture, is faithful to forgive us of all sins.

- Minister deliverance in teams, no solo acts. Allow one individual to lead while the others assist with prayer and allow another to lead as needed. Support prayer team (others) should not overshadow the leader; thus, causing confusion, competition and playing into the plans of the enemy to disrupt the deliverance ministry.

- The ministry of deliverance requires a special dose of compassion to the one being ministered to. Note: Compassion is needed for the individual not the demon being cast out. The ministry of deliverance is a ministry of compassion, love and kindness.

- The deliverance minister and helpers should not expose publicly the reason for the deliverance. Subject matter of deliverances should be kept as confidential as possible. No one wants their private, spiritual struggles exposed. Every individual should be comfortable coming for deliverance ministry. We also want to make sure we do not condemn them or judge. Those needing deliverance cannot fight demons and you too!

  This scenario will, of course, differ from public deliverance ministry services and other times, when deliverance is impromptu.

- Ministry, to frail or sickly individuals, may necessitate more than one deliverance session to enable the participant to physically withstand the deliverance. They may also need to sit while being ministered to.

- Be cognitive of how you touch individuals during ministry. Preferably women touching women, men touching men. Men should never minister to women alone and vice versa.

- Never close your eyes, be watchful when ministering deliverance and praying.

- Maintain confidence at all times. Have the "now faith".

- Individuals are never to be given advice that could result in them making wrong decision(s), (i.e. advise them to get a divorce or give advice on stock purchases, etc.).

- Do not tell but strongly recommend the removal of the "accursed things, (i.e. Ouija Board, crystal ball, etc.) from their home (s).

Order of the Deliverance Ministry

- The deliverance minister should have a brief conversation with the individual, to find out why they are there for ministry. You may want the individual receiving deliverance to complete a questionnaire and sign a release from liability waiver. The questionnaire is designed to assist the ministry team in getting to the root of the problem. Questionnaires are very helpful but the deliverance minister should always rely on guidance from the Holy Spirit. The consent form discharges the church ministry from liability and allows the individual, voluntarily coming forth for the ministry of deliverance, to assume all risk inherent with the ministry of deliverance.

- Identify the major spirit and then identify the subordinate spirits that are obeying the major spirit.

- Minister a general prayer. "Bind the powers over the area and break demonic assignments over/in the person. Ask for angelic protection (Hebrews 1:14). Ask and receive, by faith, the gifts of the spirit needed to minister". Release the power of God, the power of the blood, divine safety and the protection of Jesus for protection and safety. Source: Deliverance: The Children's Bread, John Eckhardt

- Go through the general prayers of forgiveness, repentance, rejection, etc. (see chapter 10 - Deliverance Prayers).

- In some cases, you will need to call the demon out by name. The name is usually characteristic of the behavior the individual needs deliverance from, "Lying spirit, come out".

- Cast Satan out, in Jesus' name.

- Remind demons what the word says - *"We have authority over all the power of the enemy" (Luke 10:19)*.

- Do not hold conversations with demons. These conversations are only a distraction and can hinder the deliverance process.

- Should deliverance become physically harmful to the individual, command that there be no tearing done by the spirits.

- Send every spirit into dry, desolate places "to return no more".

- Demons can be expelled from the nose and mouth, which may be accompanied by mucus, or phlegm. Bend them over/forward to ensure the individual does not choke. An individual may sit in a chair, or for shorter ministry times, stand. Before deliverance is complete, an individual may end up lying flat on the floor or be ministered to on bended knees. It is best to have an individual in the position in which the spirit is manifesting itself. Just make sure they are bent forward when they start to expel, to prevent them from choking.

- Sometimes the deliverance ministry session can get worse before it gets better (Mark 4:15, 17-19). Satan will make one last attempt to prevent the individual from receiving deliverance before he gives up (Luke 9:38). Many times, demons will hide to prevent themselves from being expelled.

- Once the individual is free, have them to praise and worship God. Also remember an individual may require more than one deliverance session.

- Give them instructions on how to keep their deliverance. Get them filled with the Holy Spirit and follow up with them. Cover deliverance ministers and individual who sought deliverance with a prayer of protection and rebuke all spirits that would try to retaliate.

Identifying Major and Subordinate Spirits by Functions

Our primary challenge, as deliverance ministry workers, is to correctly identify the strongman being used to keep people in bondage. The devil is a deceiver, whose primary goal is to kill, steal and destroy individuals, families and ministries. His primary goal during deliverance is to disguise and confuse the deliverance minister from getting at the root of the problem. If one cannot identify the root of the problem, the individual is unlikely to get free. You can start by identifying the activity associated with the bondages and then determine which strongman these activities operate under. Rely heavily on the Holy Spirit to identify those things which are secret and not overtly obvious to the onlooker, shared in a deliverance questionnaire and even unknown to the person needing deliverance. If we can identify the activity and any secret things, then we can effectively bind the strongman and his cohorts.

"Or how can one enter a strong man's house and plunder his goods, unless he first binds the strong man?" Matthew 12:29 (NKJV)

To obtain complete deliverance, (1) the strongman (leader) must be cast out and (2) its cohorts – other demons, identified by their activities and working along with the strongman, must also be cast out. Note: Distinguishing spirits by function will help to identify the strongman and the subordinates working with the strongman.

Spirit of Antichrist

Bind the antichrist spirit and loose the spirit of truth. Note the most common characteristics/manifestations used to identify the spirits working with this strongman: legalism, attacks against the Christian testimony, opposition to the children of God (church), blasphemes the Holy Spirit, opposes Gifts of the Spirit (especially tongues) blasphemes the blood of Jesus, denies the deity of Christ, teaches secular humanism, new age and the occult, opposes Christ and his teachings, denies the Atonement, suppresses ministries, encourages lawlessness, is a deceiver

Spirit of Bondage

Bind the spirit of bondage and loose liberty in Christ and the spirit of adoption. Note: The most common characteristics/manifestations used to identify the spirits working with this strongman: compulsive sin, bondage to sin, fear, anguish, addictions, bitterness, unforgiveness, spiritual blindness, fear of death, a tormenting spirit, captivity to Satan, oppression, addiction to anything, i.e., alcohol, sex, drugs or tobacco, schizophrenia, paranoia, hearing voices, hallucinations, self-mutilation

Deaf and Dumb Spirit

Bind the deaf and dumb spirit and loose the healing spirit of God. Note: The most common characteristics/ manifestations used to identify the spirits working with this strongman: insanity, seizures, epilepsy, lunatic, comatose, dumbness, mental illness, crying, foaming at the mouth, gnashing of teeth, blindness, ear problems, extreme depression or physical exhaustion

Familiar Spirit

Bind the familiar spirit and loose the Holy Spirit. Note: The most common characteristics/manifestations used to identify the spirits working with this strongman: Astrology, fortunetelling, occult, horoscope, medium, yoga, drugs, hallucinogens, passive minds, dreamers, muttering, false prophesy, clairvoyant (having the power to see things beyond natural means) and spiritualist

Spirit of Fear

Bind the spirit of fear and release the spirit of power, love and a sound mind. Look for the following characteristics/ manifestations to identify the spirits working with this strongman: Torment or horror, nightmares, worry, doubt, fears, phobias, inferiority, inadequacy, fear of the unseen, timidity, heart attacks, fear of death, anxiety, stress, fear of man, critical spirit, hermit/recluse, fear of authority, fear of failure, feeling that you never measure up

Spirit of Heaviness

Bind the spirit of heaviness/depression and loose the garment of praise and the oil of gladness. Note: The most common characteristics/manifestations used to identify the spirits working with this strongman: broken-heartedness, suicidal thoughts, inner hurts, torn spirit, excessive mourning, discouragement, lethargic, suppressed emotions, insomnia, despondency, low self-esteem, false responsibility, oversleeping, hearing voices, cutting one's self, grief, sorrow, despair, dejection, hopelessness, self-pity, loneness, gluttony, rejection, fear of the unseen, timidity, heart attacks, inner

hurts, root of bitterness, lack of praise, low self-esteem, heaviness

Spirit of Infirmity

Bind the spirit of infirmity (sickness) and loose healing. Note: The most common characteristics/manifestations used to identify the spirits working with this strongman: bent body, fever, impotent, fragileness, oppression, fear of infirmity, virus, infections, arthritis, chronic disorders, cancer, weakness, asthma, hay fever, allergies

Spirit of Jealousy

Bind the spirit of jealousy and loose the spirit of truth. Note: The most common characteristics/manifestations used to identify the spirits working with this strongman: extreme competition, anger, revenge, rage, hatred, murder, profanity, insecurity

Lying Spirit

Bind the lying spirit and release the spirit of truth. Note: The most common characteristics/manifestations used to identify the spirits working with this strongman: religious bondages, sodomy, accusations, lust, hypocrisy,

adultery, homosexuality, always opposing, profanity, church hoppers, divination, witchcraft, strong deceptions, flattery, superstitions, false prophesy, slander, gossip, lies, false teachers, whispers, foolish talking, backbiters, covenant breakers, vanity, tormenting spirits

Perverse Spirit

Bind the perverse spirit, loose the power of the Holy Spirit. Note: The most common characteristics/ manifestations used to identify the spirits working with this strongman: lust, abortion, evil actions, fornication, filthy mind, fifthly mouth, incest, child abuse, atheists, wounded spirit, pornography, sodomy, effeminate (men showing qualities attributed to women and vice versa) hates God and His WORD, self- lovers, sex perversions, twisting of the truth, wounded spirit, evil actions, foolishness, doctrinal error, contentions, quarrelsome, chronic worrier, twisting the word, inventors of evil, unholy, heresies, ungodliness,

Spirit of Pride

Bind the spirit of pride and release a humble and contrite spirit. Note: The most common characteristics/ manifestations used to identify the spirits working with this strongman: mockery, haughtiness, stubbornness, witchcraft, gossip, idleness, scornfulness, self- deception, rejection of God, arrogant, smug, self-righteous, dictatorial, controlling, over bearing, domineering, manipulation and control, rebellion, holier than thou, exalted feelings, egotistical, contentious, bragging, boastful, strife, idleness, attention seekers, interruption, impatience

Spirit of Divination

Bind the spirit of divination and release the Holy Spirit and his gifts: Note: The most common characteristics/ manifestations used to identify the spirits working with this strongman: magic power, fortuneteller, soothsayer, warlock, witch, sorcerer, rebellion, drugs (illegal or prescription) hypnotist, enchanter, stargazer and zodiac signs

Bind the spirit of error and loose the spirit of truth. Note: The most common characteristics/manifestations used to identify the spirits working with this strongman: un-submissive, false doctrine, contentious, new age movement, defensive, un-teachable, defensive, argumentative, contentions, servant of corruption, having a form of godliness, mental confusion, fears, physical illness, and pain, depression, dullness of comprehension, spiritual hindrances to prayer, bible study, listening to services, moving in the gifts of the Spirit and faith principles that have come in error

Spirit of Error

Bind the spirit of death and release life. Note: The most common characteristics/ manifestations used to identify the spirits working with this strongman: devils, mysterious forces, mythical Gods, evil wizards, magic power, accidental, random acts of violence, disease, suicide, clumsiness and fighting

Spirit of Death/ Murder

Spirit of Whoredom

Bind the Spirit of whoredom and loose the spirit of truth and the operation of the Holy Spirit. Note: The most common characteristics/ manifestations used to identify the spirits working with this strongman: unfaithfulness, adultery, prostitution, love of money, excessive appetite, worldliness, fornication, idolatry, chronic dissatisfaction

Seducing Spirits

Bind the seducing spirits and release the operation of the Holy Spirit. Note: The most common characteristics/ manifest -ations used to identify the spirits work- ing with this strongman: seared con- science, deception, fascination to evil ways, objects or persons, seducers- enticers, wanderers from the truth, hypo-critical, lies, attractions, fascinations in false prophets, signs and wonders, etc.

Source: juliagraves.tripod.com and the Deliverance manual

CHAPTER 9

Deliverance Questionnaire and Consent Form

Lest Satan should get an advantage of us: for we are not ignorant of his devices.
2 Cor. 2:11 (KJV)

Deliverance Questionnaire and Consent Form

A questionnaire is a good place to start when it comes to obtaining information about the person with whom deliverance will be provided. While there are individuals anointed enough to discern the areas where an individual might need deliverance, it's good to let the person tell you. Who, better than that individual, can tell you what they are experiencing. The Holy Spirit will confirm and maybe even show the deliverance ministry other areas the person may need deliverance. One thing we don't want to do is offend the person with information coming from our flesh. We want to minister in love. We want to do everything decently and in order and not run people away from the church or offend and bring a reproach on the Gospel.

This questionnaire will help to uncover open doors to demonic spirits. It can be instrumental in identifying the evil spirits plaguing a believer. This abbreviated deliverance questionnaire deals with 6 major areas of deliverance. Unless these areas are addressed, the individual will most likely remain bound. These areas include:

1) un-forgiveness,
2) rejection,
3) sexual sin/perversion & soul ties,
4) the occult,
5) generational curses and
6) fear.

DELIVERANCE QUESTIONAIRE

Name:

____

Address:

____

Gender: Female______ Male_______

Age________ Race_____________________

Marital Status: Married _______ Single ________

Separated ______ Widowed ________
Divorced________

# of Children and names:

____

____

____

____

____

____

____

____

____

I. BACKGROUND

1. Have you accepted Jesus Christ as your Lord and Savior? How do you know for sure?

2. Have you been baptized in water and in the Holy Spirit. How many years?

3. Are you active in church? Where do you attend church? How long have you attended this church? Where were you before?

4. Have you received Deliverance ministry before?
Yes _________ No _________

Was it successful? Yes _________ No _________

/if applicable, please elaborate.

____
____
____
____
____
____
____
____
____
____
____
____
____
____
____
____
____
____
____
____

5. Do you want and are you willing to be delivered? Are you willing to make lifestyle changes to keep your freedom?

II. CHILDHOOD

1. Did you grow up in a happy home? How was your relationship with your father, mother, grandparents, aunts, uncles, siblings, cousins, childhood friends, classmates and neighbors?

2. Did you grow up in a foster home or were you adopted? How were your relationships?

3. Describe any traumatic experiences as a child. What thing(s) impacted your life as a child (a death, rape, jail, disappointment, divorce, incest, fire, embarrassment, etc.)?

4. Are you harboring any un-forgiveness toward anyone in your family, other relationships, including God from your childhood)? List the name(s) and relationship(s).

III. ADULTHOOD

1. How would you describe your relationships with the opposite sex - (husband(s), wives(s), boyfriend(s) and girlfriend(s)?

2. Describe your relationship with your parents.

3. Describe your relationship with your siblings.

4. How would you describe your relationship with individuals from work, school or organizations of which you are involved?

5. Describe any traumatic experiences as an adult. What thing(s) have impacted your life as an adult (a death, rape, jail, disappointment, divorce, incest, fire, embarrassment, etc.)?

6. Are you harboring any un-forgiveness toward anyone in your family (family member, co-worker, boss, spouse, etc., including God)? List the name(s) and relationship(s).

IV. SEXUAL RELATIONS

1. Have you been involved in fornication (extramarital relationships, pornography, sodomy, sex while sleep, sex dreams, masturbation, prostitution, homosexuality, bestiality, group sex, pedophilia, child molestation, other)?

2. Are there any unbroken soul ties (knitting together of one's flesh with another)? Have you made any blood covenants, vows and agreements with anyone (including animals, as a child or an adult, to appease a person or commit yourself to them?)

***3.* Have you been raped or had an abortion (how many rapes/abortions)? Have you supported a spouse or girlfriend with an abortion?**

4. **Do you have a healthy sexual relationship with your spouse?**

____
____
____
____
____
____
____
____
____
____
____
____
____
____
____
____

5. Are you harboring any un-forgiveness toward anyone in your family (family member, co-worker, boss, spouse, etc., including God related to sex)? List the name(s) and relationship(s).

____
____
____
____
____

V. FEAR/REJECTION

1. What are you most tormented about in your mind (worry, stress, thoughts that you keep going over and over again?)

2. What do you fear?

3. Have you experienced rejection as a child or as an adult?

4. Have you and are you currently in a physical, sexual or mentally abusive relationship?

VI. OCCULT, BONDAGES AND CURSES

1. Have you been involved with false religions and the occult (Buddhism, Hinduism, Jehovah Witness, Mormonism, Christian Scientists, Eastern Religions, New Age, Witchcraft, Voodoo, Freemasonry, Satan Worship, Telepathy, Transcendental, Telepathy, Handwriting Analysis, Secret Societies, Pagan Religions, Religious Cults, Scientology, Martial Arts, etc.)?

____

____

____

____

2. Have you been involved in, the casting of spells, mind control, charms, voodoo, séance, fortunetelling, secret societies, astrology, tarot cards, meditation, animal/human sacrifices and rituals, mind control, levitation, crystals, mental suggestion, soul travel, water witching, automatic writing, Ouija boards, astral travel, telepathy, used LSD, marijuana, cocaine, violent videos games (Dungeons & Dragons) hypnotisms, clairvoyance, consulted a medium, ESP, tea leaves, psychics, palm readers, reincarnation teachings, spiritualist, yoga, telekinesis, extra sensory perception, occult movies, books, other supernatural experiences, etc.?

____

____

____

____

____

____

____

____

____

____

____

____

3. Do you have any cursed objects, idols or anything that could hold significance in your home?

4. Have you or are you addicted to: Smoking, food, alcohol, gambling, shopping, drugs, TV, sex, videos and other tech devices?

5. Do you have low or high self-esteem? How do you feel about yourself? Do you wallow in self-pity, self-condemnation and guilt?

6. Are you controlling, passive, compulsive or excessive, lazy or a procrastinator?

7. What behaviors do you recognize as being generational? I.e., inability to make decisions, lying, stealing, anger, violence, hurts of the past, guilt's from the past, confusion, pride, control, possessives, material lust and greed, unstable, moody, paranoia, dementia, perfectionism, problem with authority figures, rebellion, stubbornness, fear, rage, depression, suicide, dying young, unforgiveness, lust, addictions, sickness (cancer, diabetes, etc.) poverty, wealth, other, etc.

VII. DEPRESSION AND DEATH

1. Do you feel depressed, stressed, over-burdened or worried?

2. Are you taking medicines for depression or to help you sleep? Are you sleeping too much or too little?

3. Have you been hospitalized for depression or mental illness? Have you been treated for a chronic illness, disease or other physical infirmities?

4. Do you have any drug, sexual or alcohol addictions?

5. Please describe anything that has happened to you that was not asked in this questionnaire.

Deliverance Promises

Joel 2:21

King James Version (KJV)

21 Fear not, O land; be glad and rejoice: for the LORD will do great things.

Luke 4:18-19

King James Version (KJV)

18 The Spirit of the Lord is upon me, because he hath anointed me to preach the gospel to the poor; he hath sent me to heal the brokenhearted, to preach deliverance to the captives, and recovering of sight to the blind, to set at liberty them that are bruised,

19 To preach the acceptable year of the Lord.

Hebrews 2:14-15

King James Version (KJV)

14 Forasmuch then as the children are partakers of flesh and blood, he also himself likewise took part of the same; that through death he might destroy him that had the power of death, that is, the devil;

[15] And deliver them who through fear of death were all their lifetime subject to bondage.

Psalm 121:7

King James Version (KJV)

[7] The LORD shall preserve thee from all evil: he shall preserve thy soul.

Galatians 1:4

King James Version (KJV)

[4] Who gave himself for our sins, that he might deliver us from this present evil world, according to the will of God and our Father:

Genesis 45:7

King James Version (KJV)

[7] And God sent me before you to preserve you a posterity in the earth, and to save your lives by a great deliverance.

Psalm 41:2

King James Version (KJV)

[2] The LORD will preserve him, and keep him alive; and he shall be blessed upon the earth: and thou wilt not deliver him unto the will of his enemies.

Romans 10:13

King James Version (KJV)

[13] For whosoever shall call upon the name of the Lord shall be saved.

Psalm 18:17

King James Version (KJV)

[17] He delivered me from my strong enemy, and from them which hated me: for they were too strong for me.

Psalm 35:10

King James Version (KJV)

[10] All my bones shall say, LORD, who is like unto thee, which deliverest the poor from him that is too strong for him, yea, the poor and the needy from him that spoileth him?

Psalm 32:7

King James Version (KJV)

7 Thou art my hiding place; thou shalt preserve me from trouble; thou shalt compass me about with songs of deliverance. Selah.

Psalm 18:50

King James Version (KJV)

50 Great deliverance giveth he to his king; and sheweth mercy to his anointed, to David, and to his seed for evermore.

Psalm 118:17

King James Version (KJV)

17 I shall not die, but live, and declare the works of the LORD.

2 Corinthians 1:9-10

King James Version (KJV)

9 But we had the sentence of death in ourselves, that we should not trust in ourselves, but in God which raiseth the dead:

[10] Who delivered us from so great a death, and doth deliver: in whom we trust that he will yet deliver us;

Psalm 30:2

King James Version (KJV)

[2] O LORD my God, I cried unto thee, and thou hast healed me.

Joel 2:32

King James Version (KJV)

[32] And it shall come to pass, that whosoever shall call on the name of the LORD shall be delivered: for in mount Zion and in Jerusalem shall be deliverance, as the LORD hath said, and in the remnant whom the LORD shall call.

2 Timothy 4:18

King James Version (KJV)

[18] And the Lord shall deliver me from every evil work, and will preserve me unto his heavenly kingdom: to whom be glory for ever and ever. Amen.

DELIVERANCE CONSENT FORM

I do hereby affirm and state that I consent for *(Name of Ministry or Church Deliverance team)* **to administer personal ministry to me. I voluntarily participate in this prayer ministry.**

I forever release the church, pastors, prayer/deliverance team members, directors, officers, employees, agents, volunteers, contractors and representatives as well as its successors, assigned affiliates, subordinates and subsidiaries from any and all liability, actions, claims, or demands that I, my assignees, heirs, guardians, executors, administrators, spouse, next of kin and any legal representatives now or in the future, for any and all loss, damage, cost on account of injury to the person or property and/or resulting in the death of (Releasor) related to my participation in these activities, whether caused by negligence or other acts, whether directly connected to these activities or not by the releasees and the condition of the premises where these activities occur.

Deliverance Participant Signature (Releasor): ___________________________
Deliverance Ministry Witness Signature:

____

Date ___/___/_______

Source: Questionnaire model based on Church of the Harvest, Southaven, MS.

CONFIDENTIALITY FORM

I DO HEREBY AFFIRM AND STATE that I, as a participant in the Name of Ministry/Church Deliverance sessions, will not discuss, at any time, any personal information disclosed during the sessions.

Deliverance Ministry Leader

____

Date of Ministry ______________________

Participants:

1.

2.

3.

4.

5.

CHAPTER 10

Deliverance Session

And these signs shall follow them that believe; In my name shall they cast out devils… *Mark 16:17a (NKJ)*

Deliverance Session

DELIVERANCE AND PRAYER

Live a Life of Prayer

A deliverance minister/worker must spend time in prayer and/or the word before conducting deliverance sessions. Fasting is especially needed for the more difficult cases and should be done, at some point, during the week before pre-planned deliverance ministry times. Some small form of protein may be needed for individuals responsible for ministry who are physically weak on the day of ministry. Also, be sure to drink water to prevent dehydration.

The practice of prayer should be a lifestyle for the deliverance ministry worker. The success of the deliverance minister relies upon their ability to successfully engage in prayer. The Bible says, we should pray "at all times in the Spirit, with all prayer and supplication". We must be able to pray and we must be able to get our prayers through from the first heaven, through the second heaven, to the third heaven.

We must be able to get our answers to manifest in the first heaven, from the third heaven. Of course that means the answers must get through the second heaven. The second heaven is where the interference to answered prayer takes place.

The First Heaven – Where we live, what we can see with the natural eye, earth.

Second Heaven – Is the realm where angels traffic between the third heaven and earth. It is the realm where demons vigorously fight to prevent us from receiving answers to prayers.

Third Heaven – Where God dwells.

DELIVERANCE MINISTERS/LEADERS - REMEMBER TO:

- Distribute deliverance questionnaire and consent form to individual receiving deliverance prior to deliverance ministry. In addition give participant Deliverance Promises handout for them to study. It will help build their faith before day of ministry.
- Have deliverance workers complete the confidentiality form on the day of ministry.
- Pray before sessions - sweep areas clean of anything unholy, any hindering spirit that would attach itself to the person receiving deliverance, the individuals ministering deliverance or to the space where deliverance is taking place. Plead the blood of Jesus over the room and each individual in the room. Pray that there will be no transference of spirits.
- Seek angels to do battle during ministry of deliverance, use your authority, cast Satan out in Jesus' name (Psalm 91:11)
- Review the questionnaire and proceed. Please note: deliverance can take place

without a planned program, questionnaire, day or time. Remember, Jesus had no script.

- Ensure an individual is saved before ministering deliverance and is willing to forgive others. Determine if the individual wants to be saved. If not, pray a prayer of protection over the individual and send them on their way. Pray for them in your personal prayer time. Place their name on the intercessory prayer list. Pray that spiritual blindness be removed.

- At the beginning of deliverance ministry, have deliverance participant pray deliverance prayers below. Deliverance leader should then proceed to pray for the individual based on questionnaire and unction of the Holy Spirit.
- Cast Satan out in Jesus' name (Mark 16:17)
- Remind demons what the word states, we have authority over all the power of the enemy (Luke 10:19)
- Should deliverance become physically harmful to an individual, command there be no tearing done by the spirits.

- Send every spirit into dry, desolate places to return no more (Matt. 12:43)
- Once the individual is free, have them to praise and worship God. Also remember an individual may require more than one deliverance session.
- Give individual instructions on how to keep his/her deliverance. Get individual filled with the Holy Spirit and follow - up with them.
- Before and after deliverance ministry, cover deliverance workers and individual who sought deliverance with a prayer of protection and rebuke all spirits that would try to retaliate.

OTHER

- The laying on of hands is not necessary when praying. Listen to the Holy Spirit, especially if He instructs you not to touch a particular person (remember, spirits can be transferred).
- Counsel individuals on what they need to do to keep their deliverance.

BEGINNING THE DELIVERANCE SESSION

Deliverance Prayer & Confessions

Use the following prayers as a guideline at the beginning of the deliverance session. Leaders read out loud and have individual seeking deliverance repeat prayer after you. Make sure they take in deep breaths and exhale that breath after each confession prayer. We exhale because spirits are associated with breath and we want to expel all demonic activity and influence from every crevice of our bodies. This can also be achieved by yawning, crying, coughing up phlegm, deep breathing, gentle exhaling of breath, blowing of the nose or vomiting. Paper towels and waste cans should be on hand for every deliverance meeting.

Deliverance Prayers

The following prayers are to be used at the discretion of the deliverance minister. Some prayers may be added and others deleted. Every deliverance ministry is different; however, confession of sins and forgiveness is a must for all deliverances. When prayers have been prayed, deliverance leader should use the questionnaire to determine the areas that need to be prayed for.

CONFESSION OF SINS

GENERAL DELIVERANCE

FORGIVENESS

RELEASE FROM THE OCCULT

LOOSING FROM DOMINATION/BONDAGE

RELEASE FROM WITCHCRAFT

BREAKING OF CURSES

BREAKING SOUL TIES

RELEASE FROM DEPRESSION

FEAR

REJECTION

PRAISE

Confession of Sins Prayer

Lord Jesus Christ, I believe you died on the cross for my sins. I also believe that You rose from the dead so that I could be made right with the Father (Romans 4:25). You are the Son of God and You are my Savior; therefore, I refuse to hold on to sin.

I now confess all of my sins,
known and unknown, and repent of each one
(call out every known sin by name).

I ask You to forgive me and cleanse me in Your blood. Your word says, if I confess my sins, you are faithful to forgive me of my sins and cleanse me from all unrighteousness (1 John 1:9).

I accept your forgiveness. Thank You for redeeming me, forgiving my sin and cleansing me in Your blood. I declare sin has no more power over/in my life,
in Jesus' name.

GENERAL DELIVERANCE PRAYER

"I come to you, Jesus, as my deliverer.
You know all my problems –
the things that bind me, torment me, defile and harass me. I now loose myself from every dark spirit, every evil influence, every satanic bondage, every spirit in me that is not the Spirit of God and I command all such spirits to leave me now, in the name of Jesus Christ. I now confess that my body is a temple of the Holy Spirit, redeemed, cleansed and sanctified by the blood of Jesus; therefore, Satan has no place in me and no power over me, through the blood of Jesus.
In Your strength I will love, obey and serve You all the days of my life".

FORGIVENESS PRAYER

Lord, I repent for holding bad feelings against my family, friends and acquaintances.
I forgive all who I feel and know have wronged me or spoken evil of me.
I forgive every person who has ever hurt, rejected,

mistreated and disappointed

or taken advantage of me in any way.

Forgive me for not loving everyone and

holding resentment against others.

According to Mark 11:25, if I forgive others,

You will forgive me. As an act of my will, I now forgive

(name them, both living and dead (my parents, people in

the church, my pastor, my job, and

bosses and co-workers, family,

friends, ex-spouses , children)).

Lord, I bless each one of them and ask You to forgive

and release all who have hurt me. And Lord since You

have forgiven me, I also forgive myself

in the name of Jesus Christ.

I declare that I am free from the power of un-

forgiveness, in Jesus' name.

Release from the Occult Prayer (use if applicable)

I confess, as sin, and ask Your forgiveness for every occult involvement whether through ignorance or willful participation.

I confess having sought help from sources other than You, oh God. I repent and renounce all these sins and ask you to forgive me Lord. Cleanse me, spirit, body and soul. Deliver me from the powers of darkness and translate me into the kingdom of your dear Son. I renounce every occult activity

(list all occultist practices).

I renounce Satan and all his works and I put him under my feet (Psalm 8:6), knowing that Satan has no more claim on me (John 14:30). I loose myself from deceitful tongues, deceptions and lies. I renounce every oath made to man and to other false gods, in Jesus' name.

I close all doors that I have opened to the enemy. I take back all the ground I ever yielded to him. My eyes and ears are opened to the truth of the gospel of Jesus Christ. I choose Jesus as Lord of my life. I bind the spirit of

error away from me and I loose truth, and the invasion of
the Holy Spirit in my life.
I declare that the curse of the occult has
no more power over or in my life, in Jesus' name.

DOMINATION/BONDAGE PRAYER (USE IF APPLICABLE)

In the name of the Lord Jesus Christ, I renounce,
break and loose myself from all demonic influence from
individuals who attempt to control my thoughts, words
and actions.
I break all Jezebel and Ahab spirits off my life.
I break all influence from my mother, father,
grandparents and
any other human beings, living or dead,
who have dominated and controlled me in any way.
As an act of my will, I now forgive
(name them, both living and dead).
I declare that the spirit of control, manipulation
and domination has no more power in my life.

I thank You, Lord, for setting me free. I break every yoke used to keep me in bondage. I declare that I am free from all bondages and I chose to separate myself from any person or power preventing me from enjoying a spirit filled, controlled life.
I bind all the power of the enemy, strongmen, witches and all others connected demons attempting to keep me in bondage. I close the doors opened by myself and family from all hereditary curses and from all demonic bondage placed upon us as the result of sins, transgressions or iniquities through myself, my parents or any of my ancestors. I confess and repent of the sins of my forefathers. In Jesus' name, I declare that I am free.

Release from Witchcraft & Related Powers

In the name of Jesus Christ, I rebuke, break and loose myself and my family, from any and all evil curses operating through charms, vexes, hexes, spells, omens, jinxes, psychic powers, mind control,

bewitchments, witchcraft or sorcery that have been put upon me through any person or from any cult or occult source.
I break all curses of sorcery, divination, physics, tarot cards, Ouija Boards and Masonic lodges. I break all demonic powers hindering my family, finances, home, marriage, children, spirit, soul and body. I break all strongholds against my mind and emotions.
I give my mind and emotions to You Lord Jesus.
I break all addictions *(list them)* off of me, in the name of Jesus. I declare that all demonic powers have no more power over/in my life, in the name of Jesus.

Breaking Curses Prayer

In the name of Jesus Christ, I confess
all the sins of my forefathers
and by the blood of Jesus,
I break the power of every curse
passed down to me through my ancestral line.
I confess and repent of each and every sin that I have committed, known or unknown,

and accept Christ's forgiveness.
According to Galatians 3:13,
I am redeemed from the curse of the law
and no curse can operate in my life or in my family.
I break curses by generations *on*
my mother's side and father's side.
I choose the blessing and reject the curse.
I break every curse of rejection,
hurt, and broken heartedness, depression and oppression.
I break all curses of physical, sexual and verbal abuse.
In the name of my Lord Jesus Christ,
I break the power of every evil curse spoken against me.
I cancel the force of every prediction
spoken about me, whether intentionally or carelessly that
was not according to God's promised blessings. I break
all curses of words that I have spoken. I bless those who
have cursed me. In the name of Jesus, I command every
evil spirit hiding behind these curses to leave!
Go! You cannot stay! Leave me now. I declare that
curses have no more power over/in my life,
in Jesus' name. I am free.

Breaking Soul Ties/Infirmity Prayer

In the name of the Lord Jesus Christ, I renounce, break and loose myself from all demonic soul ties formed through sinful sexual encounters and
other binding agreements, contracts, oaths or blood ties.
I renounce all sexual sins including fornication, masturbation, adultery, pornography, perversion and fantasy, in Jesus name.

(Note: Be as specific as possible when breaking soul ties. Name each sexual partner, etc. and verbally renounce the soul ties with each one.)

I accept God's forgiveness for each one. In the name of Jesus, I command all demons associated with fornication, masturbation, adultery, pornography, perversion and fantasy to go.

I break all soul ties with: Animals – formed through inordinate affection for animals;
Family members – where there is control and possessiveness, incest or rape; Corrupt and depraved companions who have influenced me in perverse ways;
The dead – from prolonged mourning over deceased

loved-ones; Church related soul ties where I have been a part of church cliques, idolizing a pastor or church leader above Christ or being controlled by anyone in leadership. My body is the temple of the Holy Spirit. Satan, the Blood of Jesus is upon me, in me and it circles me. My body belongs to God. I do not want you in my life. I command all spirits of infirmities, sickness, cancer, high blood pressure, sugar diabetes, pre-mature death, itches, and arthritis (insert here chronic illness you are dealing with) to go in the name of Jesus.

I command all spirits operating in my mind to leave. Any spirits operating in my chest, stomach or wherever, I command you to leave.

I repent of the sins that opened the door.

I close the door in the name of Jesus.

Lord I thank you for setting me free!

Release from Depression Prayer

I bind the spirit of depression and oppression away from me. I pray the peace of God over my life, my mind and my circumstances. My mind is stayed on you. You said

you would keep me in perfect peace whose mind is stayed on you. I loose the spirit of peace on me, in my mind, over my circumstances. I refuse to be unsettled, agitated or upset. I cast down imaginations and every high thing that exalts itself above Christ (2 Cor. 10:5). I smash strongholds and spirits associated with depression. My sins are under the blood of Jesus and I walk in liberty. God has set me free. I bind the spirit of heaviness away from me and
I loose the spirit of praise, worship
and the oil of gladness.
I have the mind of Christ and I take back my mind, my thoughts, my peace and my joy. I declare that I am a new creation in Christ Jesus and
the joy of the Lord is my strength.

RELEASE FROM FEAR PRAYER

Lord, I confess that I have opened the doors to fear *(list the things, persons, objects that you fear)*. I know your word says, [18] There is no fear in love; but perfect love

casteth out fear: because fear hath torment. He that feareth is not made perfect in love. *1 John 4:18 (KJV)*
I refuse to be in torment and I command fear to leave me now, in Jesus name. I break the bondage of fear over me. I have the power of God, love of God and a sound mind. I will not fear death. Fear will not torment me. God you have not given me a spirit of fear, but of power, love and a sound mind. You delivered me from the spirit of fear when you died on the cross for my sins and I receive every benefit of the cross, including peace of mind and joy unspeakable and full of glory.
I receive the peace of God, which passes all my understanding and I receive the joy of the Lord, in Jesus' name.

REJECTION PRAYER AND SCRIPTURAL DECLARATIONS

Lord, even I have been rejected. I refuse to hurt or hate those who have rejected me. Instead Lord, I forgive them and ask that You cleanse me from every memory and hurt associated with these individuals.

I choose to forgive and love just as
You did on the cross when You said,
[34] Then said Jesus, Father, forgive them; for they know not what they do. Luke 23:34a (KJV)

(You)were despised and rejected of men; a man of sorrows, and acquainted with grief: ...[4] Surely (You) borne my griefs, and carried my sorrows: ...[5] But (You) were wounded for my transgressions, You were bruised for my iniquities: the chastisement of my peace was upon You; and with Your stripes I am healed (based on Isaiah 53:3-5 (KJV).

I bind every harassing spirit that keeps reminding me of my past. I halt the activities of demons who work in people who treat me as an outcast. I allow Your Holy Spirit to come into my heart and fill me with Your presence. I chose to press toward the prize which is in Christ Jesus. I declare the word of God over my life and mind. Your word says,

---

IF MY FAMILY REJECTS ME, GOD HAS MY BACK.

---

10 When my father and my mother forsake me, then the LORD will take me up. Psalm 27:10 (KJV)

I AM YOUR WORKMANSHIP OH GOD.

---

10 For we are his workmanship, created in Christ Jesus unto good works, which God hath before ordained that we should walk in them. Ephesians 2:10 (KJV)

I WAS PREDESTINED BY YOU TO BE CALLED A CHILD OF GOD

---

9 But ye are a chosen generation, a royal priesthood, an holy nation, a peculiar people; that ye should shew forth the praises of him who hath called you out of darkness into his marvellous light; 1 Peter 2:9 (KJV)

I AM A NEW CREATION IN CHRIST.

---

[17] Therefore if any man be in Christ, he is a new creature: old things are passed away; behold, all things are become new. 2 Corinthians 5:17 (KJV)

[37] Nay, in all these things we are more than conquerors through him that loved us. Romans 8:37 (KJV)

I AM AN HEIR OF SALVATION.

---

[11] In whom also we have obtained an inheritance, being predestinated according to the purpose of him who worketh all things after the counsel of his own will: Ephesians 1:11 (KJV)

I WAS CHOSEN BY GOD. I AM HOLY AND WITHOUT BLAME.

---

[4] According as he hath chosen us in him before the foundation of the world, that we should be holy and without blame before him in love: Ephesians 1:4 (KJV)

I AM AN OVERCOMER.

---

[4] For whatsoever is born of God overcometh the world: and this is the victory that overcometh the world, even our faith. 1 John 5:4 (KJV)

I AM ROOTED AND GROUNDED IN LOVE

---

[17] That Christ may dwell in your hearts by faith; that ye, being rooted and grounded in love, Ephesians 3:17 (KJV)

I AM FREE.

---

[36] If the Son therefore shall make you free, ye shall be free indeed. John 8:36 (KJV)

PRAISE PRAYER

God, I thank you for delivering me out of the hand of the enemy. I give you thanks,
in Jesus' name.
(Improvise)

Source: Based on prayers from childrenbread.net and demonbuster.com

FOR THE DELIVERANCE MINISTER/WORKER – HOW TO CALL SPIRITS OUT:

Call out the strongman and his cohorts, by name, as previously listed.

EXAMPLE: DELIVERANCE PRAYER:

Father, I bless (name) and release
your anointing on them.
In the name of Jesus Christ,
You unclean spirit, (identify strongman)
come out!
Broken heart, be healed!
Depression, discouragement, go!
I command you to leave (name) now!

Crying, wounded spirit, be healed!
(identify strongman) leave in the name of Jesus!

How to determine if an individual is free

- ✓ Take notice of the physical characteristics of the individual and determine if they are still bound. Has there been a change in their appearance?

- ✓ Ask them how they feel

- ✓ Seek confirmation from the Holy Spirit because spirits will try to make you think they are gone but they are still present.

(Repeat the steps as many times as needed, until there is complete freedom from demonic attack/possession.)

Once you have determined the person is free:

- ✓ Begin to praise God in the Spirit for the deliverance or
- ✓ Praise Him in your native tongue if you are not Holy Spirit filled

PRAYER FOR FILLING/INDWELLING OF THE HOLY SPIRIT

(To be performed after deliverance)

Heavenly Father, I ask to receive the infilling of the Holy Spirit as you have promised. Your word says, if I ask, I will receive and I ask to receive the Holy Spirit with the evidence of speaking in other tongues. In the Name of Jesus Christ, I am asking You to fill and baptize me in the Holy Spirit. Because of Your word, I believe I now receive the gift of the Holy Spirit and I thank You. I accept this gift by faith. I ask You, Holy Spirit, to rise up within me and cause me to speak with other tongues as the spirit gives me utterance.

- ✓ Begin praising God and giving sound to the expressions in your heart.
- ✓ Speak and hear the Holy Spirit speaking through you.
- ✓ Allow yourself to speak in tongues - speak, stop speaking and then start again.
- ✓ Practice speaking in the shower, driving to work, etc. You are able to stop and begin speaking in tongues whenever and wherever.

The more you step out in faith and begin to minister deliverance, the more anointed and effective you will become. Deliverance ministry that initially takes hours can subsequently take place in a matter of minutes as you grow in the areas of faith and spiritual authority. This is dependent upon the type of deliverance needed. Note: Individuals needing deliverance from such things as schizophrenia will often require several sessions. In the case of chronic illness, encourage individual to also receive medical assistance.

Common symptoms of those with an indwelling of evil spirits:

- Emotional Problems
- Mental Problems
- Speech Problems
- Sex Problems
- Addictions
- Infirmities
- Religious Error
- Pride

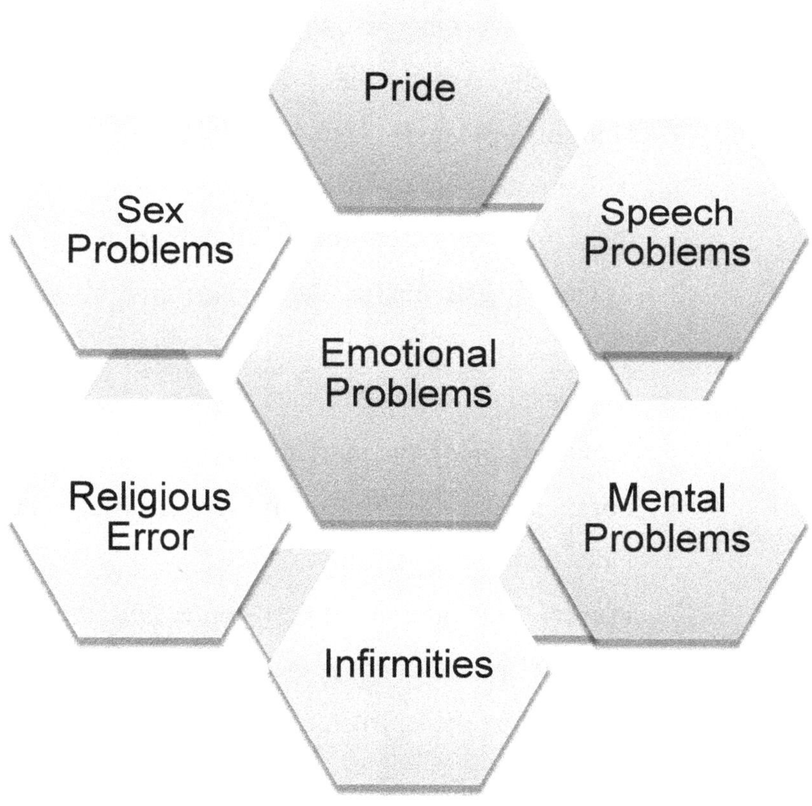
Pride
Speech Problems
Mental Problems
Infirmities
Religious Error
Sex Problems
Emotional Problems

THE STEPS TO DELIVERANCE REVIEW

1. Honesty – ensure an individual is saved before ministering deliverance
2. Humility – make sure the person wants deliverance and willingly participates. Allow them to identify areas they need help with,
3. Review questionnaire, and hear from the Holy Spirit
4. Repentance - have individual repent
5. Renunciation - have individual renounce their sin
6. Forgiveness - have them to forgive other individuals and themselves
7. Prayer – have individual pray confession prayers
8. Begin to minister deliverance

   a. Bind every spirit on assignment for each individual
9. At conclusion, pray a prayer of protection over them, if necessary, refer them to the pastors for additional ministry

SEVEN STEPS TO RETAINING YOUR DELIVERANCE

At the conclusion of the deliverance session, pray a prayer of protection over the individual going through deliverance and, if necessary, refer them to the pastor or other designated leader for additional ministry. Encourage them to do the following:

1. Put on the whole armor of God
2. Practice positive confession of the word over your life (See pages 128-129)
3. Study and apply the word to your life
4. Crucify the flesh
5. Develop a life of continuous praise and worship
6. Maintain a life of fellowship with the saints (play an active role in a local church)
7. Commit yourself totally to Christ

DELIVERANCE MINISTERS/LEADERS - REMEMBER TO:

- Bind every spirit over every assignment for each individual
- Bind every hindering spirit
- Seek assistance from angels to do battle
- Remind demons what the word says – we have authority over all the power of the enemy
- Cast Satan out in Jesus' name
- Should deliverance become physically harmful to individual, command that there be no tearing done by the spirits.
- Send every spirit into dry, desolate places to return no more
- Once the individual is free, have them to praise and worship God. Also remember, an individual may require more than one deliverance session.

- Give them instructions on how to keep their deliverance. Get them filled with the Holy Spirit and follow up with them.

- Cover deliverance ministers and individual who sought deliverance with a prayer of protection and rebuke all spirits that would try to retaliate.

FOLLOW-UP

Follow-up procedures should be established to determine whether additional deliverance is needed, whether the individual needs Godly counsel. This can be done via telephone or personal contact. Encourage individual to become spirit filled, attend Bible study, prayer and church fellowship and worship on a regular basis for growth, and encouragement in the things of the Lord.

www.ingramcontent.com/pod-product-compliance
Lightning Source LLC
Chambersburg PA
CBHW071523040426
42452CB00008B/866
* 9 7 8 0 9 9 0 5 4 4 7 0 8 *